Explore your past lives

Explore your past lives

Paul Roland

A GODSFIELD BOOK
www.godsfieldpress.com

With love and gratitude to all who have attended
my spiritual workshops and courses over the years,
and especially to those who have allowed me to
include their insights and experiences in this book.
I am particularly grateful to Tamara Mount for
permitting me to adapt 'The emotional journey'
from an original exercise that she developed as
part of her Quantum Healing therapy.

First published in Great Britain in 2005 by Godsfield Press,
a division of Octopus Publishing Group Ltd
2–4 Heron Quays
London E14 4JP

Copyright © Octopus Publishing Group 2005
Text copyright © Paul Roland 2005

Distributed in the United States and Canada by
Sterling Publishing Co., Inc.
387 Park Avenue South, New York, NY 10016–8810

1 3 5 7 9 10 8 6 4 2

Printed and bound in China

ISBN 1-84181-275-7
EAN 9781841812755

Disclaimer
The exercises in this book are intended for relaxation and increasing
self-awareness. However, if you have recently experienced mental or
emotional problems, or are taking medication, you should seek
professional medical advice before undertaking regression or practising
the exercises on your own. The author and publisher accept no
responsibility for any harm caused by or to anyone as a result of the
misuse of these exercises.

Contents

INTRODUCTION

We are constantly being told that we must live in the present and be 'mindful of the moment', for we only have one life and should live it to the full. But is that true? Although it is impossible to prove the validity of past-life experiences, the anecdotal evidence for reincarnation is overwhelming – and, by exploring your past lives, you can empower yourself to live more fully in the present.

Why explore past lives?

Once you accept the possibility that you may have experienced a succession of incarnations, you will understand that your personality and your present circumstances are not solely the result of upbringing or genetics. You will also come to realize that many of your attitudes, anxieties and aspirations as well as your behavioural traits and even health issues are an expression of those past-life experiences.

By exploring your past lives, you are no longer being a passive observer of your own life – a mere puppet at the mercy of events over which you have no control. Instead, you are becoming an active participant with the power to determine your own future.

How to benefit from this book

Even if you believe that you have no 'unfinished business' from the past to resolve, you can still benefit tremendously from the exercises and advice given in this book. It will help you become more self-aware and will empower you to take control of your destiny, by giving you all the facts you need to make the right choices. It will reveal why you hold certain beliefs, why you react the way you do to certain situations, why you encounter specific problems in life and what their purpose might be.

Once you understand the deep-seated causes of blocks and restraints in your current life, you are in a better position to make positive changes and to ensure that your future will be brighter.

Past lives, present problems

Past-life regression can help you understand the
underlying causes of present problems. It does this
by accessing suppressed memories from a previous
existence, which conventional therapy and
counselling may not address or even
acknowledge as contributory factors.

The power of regression

You may, for example, discover that you have a
difficult relationship with someone now because
you have incurred what is known as a 'karmic debt'
from a previous incarnation (see pages 92–97). Or
you may suffer from a phobia that is the result of a
traumatic experience in a past existence (see pages
73–74). In fact, many common ailments, eating
disorders, chronic complaints and even habitual
behaviour patterns may be caused by trauma in a
past life. However, you can treat them easily by
identifying the source during a regression session,
then by offering healing and closure.

In the following pages you will find a variety of
practical exercises and simple techniques for
accessing past-life memories which you can practise
on your own or with a trusted friend without having
to commit to a whole course with a regression
therapist. You may find it helpful to record
the scripts of the longer and more detailed
visualizations, as they can be difficult to memorize,
although with practice it will be sufficient to recall
the general outline of the exercise.

You will also learn how to distinguish between
genuine past-life memories and your imagination
(see page 12) and how to interpret your most
significant and puzzling dreams (see pages 48–49).
You can even use these techniques to connect with
your soul mate (see pages 64–65).

But don't embark on this exploration in the hope
that you might have been a celebrated historical
figure. It is more likely that you have lived many
mundane lives, although every one of them will have
been significant in your personal spiritual journey. It
is not *who* you were that is important, but what you
have learnt and what you can now become.

Getting started with past-life exploration

If you are seriously interested in exploring your past lives, don't be put off by the thought that you might have to take a crash course in psychology or submit yourself to a course of psychotherapy. It is quite possible to undergo regression without professional assistance, analyzing the symbolic imagery using plain old common sense. And be reassured that you can safely explore your past lives, regardless of your creed and religious beliefs. In fact many religions around the world, including Hinduism and Buddhism, incorporate reincarnation in their belief systems. Before you begin, you need to understand a few basic terms and the part they play in the process of recovering past-life impressions.

Common terms

- **Regression** Techniques used to recover memories of past lives from the unconscious mind. Many different techniques exist and will be explored in detail throughout this book.

- **Reincarnation** The embodiment of a soul in a new body.

- **The Subconscious** The region of the mind that lies just below the surface of our awareness, which we become conscious of simply by directing our attention to it. For this reason, recent memories can be recalled at will, whereas memories of our former lives may have to be recovered using techniques such as regression because they exist in the Unconscious.

- **The Unconscious** The region of the mind that we cannot access at will. It governs our instincts and impulses, and is the storehouse of our oldest memories and our deepest fears. Regression therapists work on the principle that we are able to remember beyond our birth and childhood, to our former lives. This is possible because the Unconscious is an aspect of our Higher Self, or soul, which chooses to reincarnate many times over.

Is regression safe?

Past-life regression is perfectly safe if you follow the guidelines described in this book and maintain a healthy degree of scepticism. Approach every session with an open mind and question everything you receive. Be cautious if you suspect that you are glamorizing your experiences to compensate for a sense of inadequacy or to massage a bruised ego.

You actually enter a light trance state periodically every day, though you are probably unaware you are doing so. Whenever you lose yourself in an activity that does not require you to concentrate, or recall a particularly vivid memory, you temporarily retreat into the Subconscious. The deeper you go, the more real the recollection is. Can you recall the last time you stopped at traffic lights and drifted off, reliving a pleasant memory – only to be startled back to everyday awareness by the horn of the car behind you? That was involuntary regression. Past-life regression is just one step further back. With practice, you will be able to enter a light trance state as effortlessly as you refocus on an object close to you after focusing on one some distance away.

If you find yourself becoming preoccupied with the details of a past life, or relating differently to other people because you believe there may be a karmic connection between you, stop the regression sessions

immediately. And you should never practise self-hypnosis and self-awareness exercises if you suffer from mental strain or are under the influence of alcohol or drugs (prescribed or otherwise). If you are anxious about your fitness to try regression, consult your doctor, therapist or counsellor. However, in general, past-life exploration is safe and frequently proves both beneficial and illuminating.

Useful tips

- Limit your regression sessions to half an hour (or an hour at the maximum), no more than twice a week.

- Affirm your commitment to the present by practising the grounding exercise (see page 40) at the end of each session.

- If you are still restless to expand your awareness, practise meditation (up to twice a day, every day) to quieten your mind, and visualization (for up to half an hour, every day) to strengthen your connection with the Unconscious.

Things to remember

- Past-life regression is for greater self-awareness – not for escapism or to fuel a personal fantasy.

- Stay detached and rational; gather the facts and do not be in a hurry to come to a conclusion.

Why you do not remember your past lives

Generally you are unlikely to remember your past lives without help in retrieving them. However, memories of previous relationships will begin to surface if you actively seek out answers that may lie in a former life. If you are considering how a past life might be influencing the present, this suggests that you have reached a state of maturity and self-awareness where you are ready to assimilate these experiences and not let them disturb your relationships with the relevant people.

Reasons for forgetting

You may have chosen to forget your past lives for a number of reasons, the main one being that you need to begin each life with a clean slate so that your attitude to other people is not coloured by previous relationships. Imagine how awkward it would be if you remembered that your partner had been your parent in a previous existence, or that your employer had been your servant. Human relationships are complicated enough, without adding into the equation factors from past lives.

Another reason why you choose not to remember is that the strongest, most readily recalled memories are often negative ones. You would be unable to function in your new life if you were burdened with resentment, regrets and guilt as the result of your actions in a previous existence. Your mind, which is geared to self-preservation, automatically suppresses negative experiences, while other experiences are readily forgotten because each is largely indistinguishable from another.

Another significant factor in forgetting is the process that occurs after death. Between lives you exist in a state similar to that which you experience during sleep. In this period of rest and regeneration you become detached from the life led by your former persona – just as in the morning you relinquish your dreams, which at the moment of experiencing them seemed so real and significant.

How past-life memories can be recovered

Professional regression therapists rely on hypnosis to recover past-life impressions, but there are various simple, effective techniques that you can try safely on your own without supervision. These involve working with your dreams, using symbolism, journaling, drawing, psychometry, using sounds and scents, meditation and visualization, all of which are described in detail in the relevant sections of this book.

The author's story

I experienced an example of involuntary past-life recollection some years ago during a meditation. In a moment of calm, when no thoughts could intrude, an image spontaneously appeared and took on a life of its own. I found myself in a room surrounded by Jewish rabbinical scholars, who were congratulating me on some achievement.

This was not a product of my imagination as I could not manipulate the image in any way. I could only observe it through the eyes of my former self as the scene played itself out. But the most striking aspect was the fact that each person in the 'vision' was a fully formed and distinctive personality – a feat that it would have been beyond the ability of my imagination to create.

Accessing the Unconscious

Ultimately you will begin to experience involuntary glimpses into your past lives once you have reached an advanced state of awareness and have opened the Third Eye (see page 41). At this stage images can occur spontaneously during moments of relaxation or extreme fatigue. You will only have to close your eyes to tap into the reservoir of memories stored in the Unconscious. Once you become 'open' to these impressions, you may trigger involuntary recall through a particular piece of music or a fragrance associated with a significant event in a previous life.

Memory or imagination?

If there is one question that nags at even the most fervent believer in the past-life phenomenon it is: 'How can I be certain that what I see during a regression session, or in a meditation, is a genuine memory and not a product of my imagination?' Well, it is actually surprisingly simple to distinguish between the two.

Genuine memory attributes

The image is likely to be genuine if it appears spontaneously and not as the result of a suggestion made by a therapist. If the image is sustained, without any conscious effort on your part, and you cannot manipulate it at will, you can be confident it is a genuine memory or a significant communication from the Unconscious. And if the image has a life of its own, so that you find yourself observing it as you would watch a movie, then it is certainly a past-life impression.

In the majority of past-life recollections you will have a first-person perspective – as if looking through the eyes of the person you were at that period in time. But don't worry if you find yourself being a witness to your own death in a previous incarnation. This third-person perspective does not mean that the image is a product of your imagination: the phenomenon is possible because this memory comes from your Higher Self, which detaches itself at the moment of death. It is the last image of that life that you take with you, so it is quite common for it to be the first image you recall when you initially open up to past-life recollections.

Things to remember

- There is no need to be anxious if you find yourself observing your own death or another unpleasant incident – these are mental images and rarely elicit any emotional response.

- If you do become emotional, don't suppress your emotions, as you clearly need to work through this episode.

What are your reasons for exploring your past lives?

Before you begin your exploration, take a moment to consider why you want to start this process and what you are looking for. Having some insight into your motives will help focus your search on aspects of your past lives that are most beneficial to your current concerns. It can also stimulate the flow of past-life information from your subconscious awareness.

You might find it useful to create a past-life journal (see page 46) in which you note your answers to the questions below and other exercises in this book. Reading over your responses may trigger additional associations and provide insights that you would otherwise miss.

1 What do you currently believe happens after death? How does this view compare to your childhood beliefs, and to those of your family and friends? Are you satisfied with your current views, or are you looking for a new perspective?

2 Have you ever wondered why you were born into your family, why you chose your partner, or why you have the children you do? What is it about each relationship that seems unusual or makes you curious?

3 Jot down any people you have met who it seems you already knew. Note whether you experienced an instant attraction or an instant dislike. How might a better understanding of the reasons for your reaction improve the relationship?

4 Make a list of any physical symptoms or emotional problems you have that you would like to understand better. How might comprehending the causes of your problems help you to resolve them?

5 List any places you have visited or learnt about, historical periods or

events, or unusual hobbies or interests, to which you feel particularly drawn. How do you explain your interest?

6 Make notes to remind yourself of any particularly vivid dreams you have had. What is it about these dreams that you would like to understand better?

7 Are you afraid of dying? Would it comfort you to know that after this life you might live again? Why (or why not)?

8 Read over your answers. What do they reveal about your reasons for exploring your past lives?

HOW CAN I BE SURE I HAVE LIVED BEFORE?

Although many people around the world believe in past lives, it is sometimes hard for those who have not been raised with this belief to accept unconditionally that they have lived before. Doubts about the reality of past lives can slow down the flow of past-life memories and make your exploration more difficult.

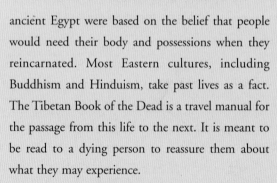

Looking at the evidence

This chapter invites you to consider the question 'How can I be sure I have lived before?' It presents three kinds of evidence of past lives for you to think about. Though the examples here may not convince you beyond doubt that you have lived before, they can help you check your beliefs against what others have thought, and gain clarity about your own views.

The first type of evidence comes from *research and scientific studies*. Psychic researchers, including respected university scientists, have collected many accounts of past-life memories from adults and children. When the researchers investigated the historical accuracy of these memories, they were astonished at their uncanny reliability. As you will see, spontaneous recall of past-life memories, especially by children, is strong evidence for reincarnation.

The second type of evidence is drawn from *past and current beliefs of world cultures*. The pyramids, mummies and richly appointed burial chambers of ancient Egypt were based on the belief that people would need their body and possessions when they reincarnated. Most Eastern cultures, including Buddhism and Hinduism, take past lives as a fact. The Tibetan Book of the Dead is a travel manual for the passage from this life to the next. It is meant to be read to a dying person to reassure them about what they may experience.

Finally, you will read accounts of *out-of-body experiences (OBEs)* and *near-death experiences (NDEs)*. Stories from people who have nearly died, or who have died and been resuscitated, as well as accounts of spontaneous out-of-body events, are strong evidence that the soul can separate from the body and may do so at death – either to return to its original home or to seek a new one.

Research and scientific studies

The research that has been undertaken into the subject of reincarnation offers a good way of validating the subject. The popular concept of reincarnation is that you are reborn with the same basic personality, but in a different body. But if you have indeed lived before, would you really think and feel the same as you do today? Could it be that a different aspect of your personality comes to the fore in your next life?

Different times, different personalities

This is a possibility raised by experiments conducted in the 1970s by the British hypnotherapist H. W. Hurst. After regressing a group of volunteers, he subjected each of them to a series of psychological tests. He then compared the results with those obtained using the same tests while his subjects were fully conscious. The results led Hurst to conclude that when he regressed each person to a previous life, they became a 'totally different person'.

To verify his findings he submitted his data to two independent psychologists, who agreed that, when comparing character traits, there was on average remarkably little similarity (just 23 per cent) between the volunteers' past and present personalities.

Perhaps we should not be surprised by this, because many subjects exhibit infantile behaviour and reflexes when they are regressed to childhood. Stage hypnotists are often accused of misusing their powers of suggestion to force their subjects into making fools of themselves and acting out

of character. However, in a therapeutic situation, hypnosis appears to awaken the child within. The subject will regress to using childish vocabulary and, if asked to write or draw, will produce work that reproduces the style they had at the suggested age. More remarkably, subjects who were born left-handed and trained to use their right hand in order to conform, will instinctively write with their left hand, although they have no conscious memory of having ever been left-handed.

After the success of such experiments, hynotherapists saw the potential for using hypnosis to delve deeper into the Unconscious and unearth memories from a patient's former lives.

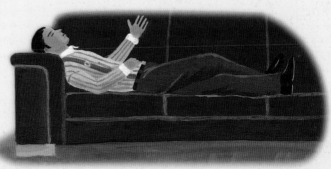

Free will or fate?

One of the most frequently asked questions concerning reincarnation is whether you have any choice in determining who you will be in your next life. The scientific evidence suggests that you do.

Choosing your next incarnation

For more than 50 years Dr Ian Stevenson, chairman of the Department of Psychiatry at the University of Virginia and a past president of the British Society for Psychical Research, has investigated numerous cases of reincarnation. Several of these appear to prove that the soul transcends gender and we can choose to return as male or female – and to determine who our parents will be.

Stevenson cites the case of a Brazilian girl, who at the age of two-and-a-half astonished her parents by recalling incidents from the life of her mother's best friend, Maria de Oliveiro, who had died at the age of 28. The child claimed that Maria had suffered two failed relationships and had committed suicide by deliberately contracting tuberculosis. Both assertions were true. Stevenson then meticulously documented more than a hundred incidents in which the child correctly identified Maria's acquaintances or made significant references that were later verified. However, the most astonishing aspect was the little girl's unshakeable assertion that, as Maria, she had promised to return as her best friend's daughter and wanted it known that she had fulfilled her promise.

A fisherman keeps his promise

In North America, Tlingit fisherman William George promised his son that if he departed this life prematurely he would return as his own grandson, and that he would bear specific birthmarks to indicate that he had kept his promise. Shortly thereafter William drowned. A year later, in May 1950, his daughter-in-law gave birth to a son who bore the exact birthmarks William had described. The boy soon displayed certain mannerisms that were characteristic of his grandfather and identified the old man's watch, although he had never seen it before.

Other evidence for reincarnation

Some of the most compelling evidence of reincarnation has been offered by children who have been able to describe their former lives in considerable detail, including events of which they could have had no conscious knowledge at their age. What makes these cases even more remarkable, and worthy of scientific investigation, is the fact that their stories have been verified by the very same people with whom they claim to have lived in their previous existence.

The receptivity of children

It is thought that children retain memories of their former lives more readily than adults because they still have a strong, unrestricted connection with the Unconscious. It is only after the age of five that 'the veil comes down', grounding them in the 'real world' and weakening their memories of past lives.

A curious aspect of these cases is that many involved the subject's violent death – and this trauma may have been a contributory factor in their ability to recall the incident. However, the most intriguing point is the 'physical evidence': birthmarks that resemble the scars you might expect to find if the fatal wounds had healed.

For example, a six-year-old Indian boy named Ravi Shankar described being beheaded in his previous life by a jealous relative, who had murdered him for his property. Not only was the scenario an unlikely subject for a child's fantasy, but an unmistakable knife-shaped scar on Ravi's neck appeared to support his claim.

Another child, Jimmy Svenson of Alaska, recalled a previous existence as his own uncle, who had died in suspicious circumstances. Jimmy was only two years old when he first mentioned this former life to his startled parents, who were disconcerted to discover birthmarks on their son's abdomen that bore a marked similarity to bullet wounds.

A further compelling case was that of a Sinhalese boy, Wijeratne, who had been born with a deformed arm. At the age of two the child claimed that his deformity was a punishment for having killed his wife in his former life, when his name had been Ratran Hami. When questioned some years later, Wijeratne was able to describe the circumstances that had led to the crime; the weapon that Ratran had used; and the argument that he gave in his defence at his trial. All these points were subsequently

A verbal clue

To the consternation of his parents, three-year-old David lay on the lounge floor and declared that was how he looked when he died. They might have laughed the incident off as a child's fantasy, had he not added that it was then that he went 'through the gate'. After some research, David's parents discovered that 'going through the gate' was an archaic expression peculiar to a particular religious sect to which his grandparents had belonged 100 years earlier.

confirmed. Even after Ratran's conviction and execution, the facts of the case were still disputed between those who believed that Ratran had accidentally stabbed his wife in a struggle and those who maintained that he had murdered his wife in a fit of temper. The child's 'confession' appeared to settle the matter.

The case of Shanti Devi

Perhaps the most convincing case of past-life recall on record is that of Shanti Devi, a young Hindi girl whose past-life recollections became the subject of intense study by the American Society for Psychical Research.

Extraordinary evidence

In 1923 three-year-old Shanti began regaling her parents with stories about her life with her husband and children, but they dismissed them as a childhood fantasy. By the time she was seven, Shanti had sketched in her stories with considerable detail; this included the names and description of her family, the name of the town (Muttra) and the fact that she had died in 1925, giving birth to a fourth child.

She claimed that her name had been Ludgi and that her husband was called Kedarnath. Although the town she named did in fact exist, Shanti's parents were concerned for her sanity and consulted a doctor. He was stunned to hear her describe medical procedures that a child could not possibly have known of. Then fate took a hand.

An acquaintance of Shanti's father called unannounced, and the girl immediately greeted him as her husband's cousin. The man confirmed that he lived in Muttra and that he did in fact have a cousin called Kedarnath, whose wife Ludgi had died in childbirth.

Without informing their daughter, Shanti's parents then arranged for Kedarnath to call, but she recognized and identified him immediately. She then became the subject of a rigorous scientific investigation by the Indian government, and was taken to Muttra for the first time by a team of researchers. She was led blindfold through the town and, after having had the blindfold removed, was able to take them straight to Ludgi's house. There she was reunited with her children, as well as her husband's parents and brother, all of whom Shanti correctly identified. The only person she failed to recognize was the fourth child, whom she had died giving birth to.

On a subsequent visit to the town, to see the house of Ludgi's mother, Shanti commented upon the changes that had been made to the house since her death. She then led investigators to the place where Ludgi had hidden her jewellery. Not even her husband had known it was buried there.

Reincarnation and religion

For thousands of years different religions all over the world have accepted the existence of past lives. Burial rites and spiritual beliefs in Tibet, and in ancient Egypt and Greece, which passed to early Christianity, are based on the understanding that we have lived before and will live again. Reading about these practices can help you clarify your own views on reincarnation.

The Tibetan Book of the Dead

Of the many accounts written in ancient times about the process of life and death, the most illuminating is arguably the Tibetan Book of the Dead. It was written to allay the anxieties of the dying, and to guide them through the various stages that determine whether they would attain Nirvana (freedom from the cycle of reincarnation) or be reincarnated.

The text takes the form of instructions to the deceased, to be recited at the time of death and on 49 successive days – the maximum time during which the soul is believed to hover nearby in the intermediate state between death and rebirth, known as *bardo*.

Though written approximately a thousand years ago, the accounts of the three stages of death are strikingly similar to recently reported near-death experiences (see page 27) that have been described by people of varying backgrounds and beliefs. But Tibetans believe that such states of awareness (unlike the Judaeo-Christian concept of heaven) are projections of the mind, similar to the dream-state in which the deceased creates their own heaven or hell, according to their expectations.

The three stages

The first stage, which the Tibetans call *chikai bardo*, is the moment when the physical functions have ceased, but the person remains conscious, unaware that they are dead. A moment later they find themselves floating free of their body, but unable or unwilling to leave the physical world behind.

Even then emotional attachments may cause the soul to linger, especially if it has a strong desire to remain with family or friends. But eventually it must enter and be absorbed by the 'clear, primordial light'. The assumption is that if a person has experienced the light during their lifetime, they will not be afraid when drawn to it after death. This belief recalls the main theme of many near-death experiences, in which the 'dying' person feels an irresistible attraction to the light and a reluctance to return to their physical body, with which they no longer identify.

For those who are unprepared to surrender to the light, or who are still emotionally bound to the physical world, this prospect is terrifying and they retreat through a succession of dream-like states of their own making.

If they pass through the light, the next stage is a judgement – a common feature of many religions, although here it is clearly intended to convey the idea that the deceased will be judged by their own conscience:

... the Good Genius, who was born simultaneously with thee, will come now and count out thy good deeds [with] white pebbles, and the Evil Genius, who was born simultaneously with thee, will come now and count out thy evil deeds [with] black pebbles ... Then the Lord of Death will say, 'I will consult the mirror of Karma.' So saying, he will look in the mirror, wherein every good and evil act is vividly reflected.

The 'Lords of Death' are also seen as fearful imaginings, described in the Book of the Dead as 'thine own hallucinations'.

Having faced the consequences of their actions, the deceased can then appeal to the compassion of the Buddha. But if they cannot convince the Divine, they must reincarnate. This is the most perilous stage, for after the ecstasy of liberation from the body, the soul must now enter the cold clay of flesh and experience the trials of life once more. For many souls, the fear of remaining in the limbo of *bardo* is greater than that of reincarnating, forcing them to make an impulsive choice. The concluding prayers of the Book of the Dead are intended to guide the soul to a favourable incarnation.

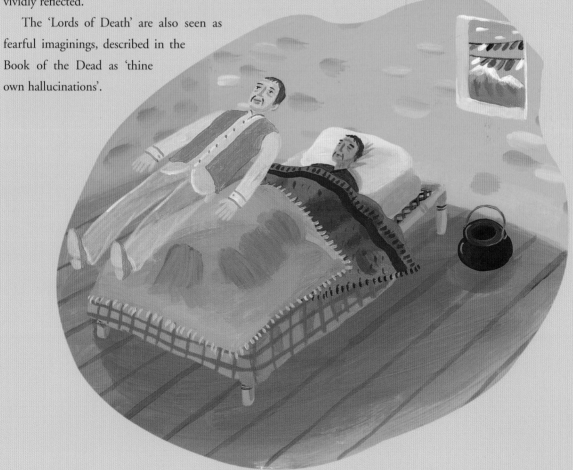

Ancient Egypt

Ancient Egyptians may have been the first people to accept the idea of past lives. Herodotus, the Greek historian who lived in the fifth century BCE, wrote that the Egyptians were the first to teach that the human soul is immortal. They believed that, after death, the soul spends three thousand years being reborn in the bodies of all creatures of land, sea and air, before being born again in a human body. As it passes through these many lives, the soul grows in wisdom and understanding. The idea that the soul passes through various animal lives before being born in human form is called 'transmigration'.

The cult of Osiris

More details about the beliefs of the ancient Egyptians has come from archaeological evidence uncovered in tombs. Objects, inscriptions and paintings connect Egyptian beliefs in reincarnation to the mystery cult of Osiris, an Egyptian god who himself died and was resurrected.

Ancient texts describe Osiris as one of the judges before whom a soul has to appear after death. After passing through dangers such as monsters, boiling lakes, fires and snakes, the soul comes to a judgement hall, where Osiris presides. The heart of the deceased is placed on one side of a balance scale. On the other side is the white feather of Truth, which holds all the lies and sins of the person's life. If a person has led a decent life, the heart passes the test, and the person is judged worthy of eternal life. If it fails, the soul returns to earth to be reborn in a succession of lives until its lessons are learnt.

Egyptian burial customs and funeral rites were also based on an acceptance of past and future lives. Egyptians believed that, in order to enjoy the afterlife, a person's human identity had to be preserved. To protect the body, it was made into a mummy. In the process, all of the organs were removed, except for the heart, which would be weighed in the judgement hall of Osiris.

High-ranking Egyptians were buried in elaborate tombs, on which the name of the deceased was inscribed. Food, drink, furniture and other precious objects were placed in the tomb for the person to use in the afterlife. To protect the spirit of the deceased, inscriptions were written on the sarcophagus that held the mummy, on the tomb walls, and on papyrus or linen scrolls placed in the tomb. These

texts often included the story of the death and resurrection of Osiris, and spells to protect the deceased on the dangerous journey ahead.

The teachings pass to the Greeks

Egyptian beliefs about the journey of the soul after death are thought to have passed next to the ancient Greeks. The Greek philosopher and mathematician Pythagoras, who lived in the sixth century BCE, spent some time in Egypt studying its philosophy. Often called the father of reincarnation, Pythagoras taught that the soul goes through a series of rebirths. Between death and rebirth, it rests and is purified in the underworld. As the result of a series of rebirths, the soul is so purified that it can leave the cycle of reincarnation.

The Greek belief is echoed in early Christian teachings. An early Christian writer, St Gregory, Bishop of Nyssa (331–395 CE), wrote that the soul needed to be healed and purified, which could happen either in one life on earth or in a series of earthly lives. Later, in 533 CE, reincarnation was declared a heresy by the Council of Constantinople.

As we saw in the previous section, Eastern philosophy also has extensive teachings about what happens to a person's soul after death. As you read about the beliefs of other cultures, note whether these ideas help you to be sure that you have lived before.

Experiential evidence for past lives

 While science has yet to offer conclusive proof of the existence of the human soul and its survival after death, there is overwhelming and compelling experiential evidence obtained from people who claim to have had out-of-body and near-death experiences. These experiences suggest that death is merely a transitional stage between this life and the next.

Out-of-body experiences

Have you ever dreamt you were floating above the ground or flying across the oceans, and then realized that you were no longer dreaming? Maybe you dreamt that you were falling, just before you woke?

If so, you had what is known as an 'out-of-body experience' (OBE) – a far more common phenomenon than you might imagine. Various surveys suggest that as many as one person in five has a clear recollection of such an experience. However, it is possible that everyone experiences an OBE at some point in their life, but that many dismiss it as a dream or fail to realize its significance.

If such subjective experiences are real, they would seem to prove the existence of the 'subtle body' (also known as the etheric, dream or astral body) that explains how reincarnation is possible. If you can project your consciousness beyond the physical body, is it not likely that this immortal aspect survives death and can choose to occupy a new body in order to gain further experience? OBEs therefore offer strong evidence that we may have lived before and can live on after death. However, to many the real significance of an OBE is more personal and profound – freeing them from the fear of death and the unknown.

Ingo Swann's OBE

An involuntary OBE was experienced by the celebrated American psychic Ingo Swann, who at the age of two-and-a-half floated free of his body and watched as a surgeon removed his tonsils. When Swann regained consciousness he was able to describe the operation and show his astonished parents where the surgeon had placed his tonsils (in a jar hidden from view, behind rolls of tissue). As an adult, Swann was able to leave his body at will to view pictures placed on a platform above his head, during a series of experiments at Stanford University in the 1960s.

The subtle body and the soul

It is believed that the subtle body and the soul are two distinct entities. The soul is our Divine Essence and the subtle body is the matrix of psychic or etheric energy surrounding it. This serves as a vehicle allowing us to descend through the denser worlds from the Divine Realm to our physical world.

Cross-cultural beliefs

The belief that we all possess a soul, or 'spirit double', is common to 57 contemporary cultures and has been the central concept in numerous religions and philosophies since ancient times. The Egyptians speak of the Ka, which they identify as one of three spirits of increasing density. Each subtle body was thought to form a protective skin around the soul as it descended through the upper worlds into matter.

The Greeks too believed in the existence of the soul, which they called a 'daemon' – a term since corrupted to denote an evil spirit. And the Romans acknowledged the existence of the 'genius', a term used to denote each person's immortal Higher Self.

The return of Karin Page

Spiritual healer Karin Page had an experience at the age of 28 that convinced her of the existence of life after death. 'I had been taken to hospital suffering from pneumonia, but was fully conscious and acutely aware that what I was experiencing was not a dream. As I lay alone in the ward I drifted out of my body towards the ceiling and looked back to see myself lying in the bed. At that moment the nurse came in, noticed that I was in trouble and called the doctor. I could see what was going on, but I couldn't hear what they said. I was cosseted in a warm stillness. It was utter peace, bliss, joy, release. I wasn't concerned at all for the body lying in the bed, as I intuitively knew it wasn't the real me. Then I became aware of a brilliant light above me, which was drawing me upwards. I wanted to go on into the light, but something drew me back. A moment later I had snapped back into my body. From that moment I lost my fear of death and intuitively knew that all would be well.'

How to induce an OBE

If you want incontrovertible proof of the existence of the subtle body – and therefore of its ability to move on to a new life – you can induce an OBE and experience for yourself the exhilaration of floating free of your physical body.

1   Lie flat on your back, with your arms loosely by your sides and your head supported on a pillow. Relax and sense your body becoming lighter with every exhalation.

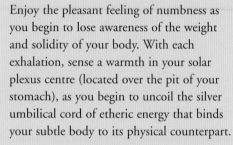

Enjoy the pleasant feeling of numbness as you begin to lose awareness of the weight and solidity of your body. With each exhalation, sense a warmth in your solar plexus centre (located over the pit of your stomach), as you begin to uncoil the silver umbilical cord of etheric energy that binds your subtle body to its physical counterpart.

2   Feel the warmth spreading across your stomach and permeating your lower back, easing any tension and resistance caused by anxiety or stress. If you have any emotional blockages caused by unpleasant memories of your birth, or connected with your death in a previous life, this will release them.

3   Now focus again on your breathing and, with each exhalation, sense that you are forming a cushion of etheric energy under your body. You can float away on this and leave your problems behind.

4   Feel yourself rising from the floor, safe in the knowledge that you are secured by the silver umbilical cord.

5   Remember that you are in control at all times and can return to your body at will.

Near-death experiences

Near-death experiences (NDEs) are the best evidence for reincarnation that we have at present. They are often confused with out-of-body experiences because both involve projection of the subtle body. However, in an OBE the individual is confined to the physical dimension, whereas in an NDE he or she passes through a tunnel of light into a higher state of existence (often alluded to as the 'heavenly realm').

Survival evidence

The first serious scientific study of this phenomenon was conducted in the 1970s by Dr Raymond Moody, an American physician who collected and compared 150 first-hand accounts – many of them from people who were resuscitated after being declared clinically dead. To Moody's astonishment, the descriptions were uncommonly consistent, despite the fact that his subjects came from diverse backgrounds and did not have the same beliefs. Some had even been sceptical of so-called 'survival evidence', and yet they described strikingly similar episodes, identified common elements and were all profoundly affected by their experience.

In almost every case the moment of death was painless and accompanied by an overwhelming sensation of peace. Many patients described the sense of liberation they felt on floating free of their physical body. Several were even able to describe in detail the procedures used to revive them, which were subsequently verified by medical staff.

While they were in the astral or etheric state, many subjects could hear what the doctors or paramedics were saying to each other, although no

The case against NDEs

The medical establishment dismisses NDEs as hallucinations, caused by a lack of oxygen in the dying brain or by the side-effects of drugs. But hallucinations are random, illogical and abstract – unlike NDEs, which are remarkably consistent. Moreover, during an NDE the individuals are acutely aware of what they are experiencing and lucidly describe a sense of heightened reality, not a confused dream-like state. Furthermore, hallucinations are not possible when the brain is inactive, which is its state during NDEs.

one appeared to be aware of the subject's presence; nor could they get anyone to hear them when they urged the doctors to let them go. In almost every case the subject suffered intense regret on being drawn back into their body, as well as experiencing a palpable sense of loss for something that they knew to be awaiting them at the end of the tunnel of light.

Between lives

Assuming that we do not pass from one life straight into the next, there must be a state in which we rest, perhaps in order to process our experiences before undertaking our next incarnation. But could there really be a state of bliss – a paradise – as promised by the major world religions? Or is this merely wishful thinking? If the numerous accounts of near-death experiences are to be believed, such a state is part of a greater reality – more real, in fact, than our physical world.

The 'in-between' place

So, what actually happens to the soul after the death of the body? As previously stated, Buddhists believe that the soul leaves the body at the time of death and passes into an 'in-between' place, or *bardo*. In most traditions, the *bardo* is at best a disorienting place, and at worst a fearful one. A soul's *bardo* experience is determined by the kind of life the person led. Lives that are characterized by negative emotions (such as greed, jealousy and hatred) lead to a fearful *bardo* experience, in which the disembodied consciousness confronts nightmare-like apparitions.

Buddhists believe that the *bardo* lasts from seven to forty-nine days, after which the soul dies to its *bardo* existence and takes rebirth. The fortunate soul of a person who has lived a virtuous life will take rebirth in a human body. One version of events holds that the soul is drawn to the place where its future parents are making love, and enters human form at the moment of conception.

An unfortunate soul, on the other hand, may take rebirth in one of the other realms of existence – the hell realms, the hungry-ghost realm, the animal realm, the realm of the jealous gods or the realm of the long-lived gods. The sixth realm, the human realm, is considered fortunate, because conditions here are conducive to spiritual progress. Unlike the Christian hell, a rebirth in the hell realm (or any other) is only temporary. The soul continues to die and be reborn in any of the realms propelled by its past deeds (known as karma, see page 92) until it has sufficient spiritual development to achieve Nirvana, the state of perfect freedom from which no rebirths are necessary.

The most fortunate souls are reborn in a Pure Land, an ideal place not unlike the Christian heaven, where conditions are perfect for the soul to continue its spiritual growth.

Witnessing the 'other side'

One of the most vivid descriptions of the heavenly dimension was recorded by American psychic researcher David Wheeler, who included the case in a survey on the subject entitled *Journey to the Other Side* (1977). The subject, whom Wheeler identified as Kenneth G., suffered a fatal heart attack shortly after being admitted to hospital. 'He was as dead as anyone I have ever seen,' commented the doctor who tried to revive him. But Kenneth G. recovered, with no ill-effects or brain damage, thereby defying orthodox medical opinion. However, the most remarkable aspect of the case was the description given by the miracle patient of 'the other side'.

Passing through a tunnel of light, Kenneth G. emerged in a verdant valley of low hills and rolling plains, floating gently down to land in a meadow of tall grass. In the distance he caught a glimpse of dense forests inhabited by grazing animals. And all around grew a profusion of exotic flowers.

Then he heard a voice urging him not to be afraid, which he recognized as that of his father, who had died ten years earlier. The next moment he was drawn to the sound of laughing children as they played in a park across the meadow. Kenneth G. was astonished to see that they were his old playmates: 'I was a little boy again, reliving [my] youth ... God, it was beautiful!'

Kenneth G.'s description of this celestial garden is typical of those reported by people who claim to have had an NDE. It cannot be readily dismissed as the result of cultural conditioning – they agree on so many details that it is difficult to argue against the suspicion that they have visited the same place. For all of them there was a sense of recognition and a feeling that they had 'come home'.

Have you lived before? 20 clues to your past lives

Answer the following questions honestly and without pre-judging your responses.

1   Do you have an enduring fascination with a particular period in history?

2   Do you feel drawn to a specific location with which you have no conscious connection?

3   Have you ever sensed that 'home' is somewhere else?

4   Have you ever felt that you were living in the 'wrong time', and that you didn't belong in the present?

5   Have you ever had dreams set in the distant past, which seem too real to be mere dreams?

6   Do you have an unusually strong emotional bond to a friend, family member or acquaintance, which cannot be explained by your present relationship?

7   Do you feel an inexplicable enmity towards someone you know, without understanding why you dislike or distrust them?

8   Is there a piece of music that stirs your emotions with a longing for a place and era that you feel is 'lost' to you?

9   Are there any persistent physical ailments or health issues for which you are unable to find a physical cause?

10 Do you suffer from a phobia or irrational fear for which you can find no obvious cause?

11 Do you sometimes have access to knowledge you couldn't have acquired in your present life?

12 Are you 'wise beyond your years', or have you ever been called 'an old soul'?

13 Do you have a hunger for exploring past lives, which is much more than mere idle curiosity?

14 Do you suspect that you deserve more than you have, and that your present circumstances may have been determined by something beyond your influence?

15 Are you distrustful of people in general and fearful for your safety and security, although there is no logical reason for your anxiety?

16 Do you have a love for antiques and historical buildings, which you suspect might be due to more than their aesthetic beauty?

17 Do your hobbies and interests reflect an interest in the past that might be considered unusual for your age?

18 Do you have an uncommonly strong interest in another culture?

19 When you were a child did you demonstrate abilities, understanding and knowledge that were unusual for someone of your age?

20 As a child did you ever refer to another home or family?

If you answered 'yes' to fewer than three questions, it suggests that you may have unconsciously suppressed memories of your past incarnations, because you have been conditioned to deny that such things are possible. Or you may simply be so preoccupied with the present that you have never given the idea serious thought. You may have had a vague feeling from time to time that certain places were familiar, despite never having been there; or you may have had other hints, such as those described above, but dismissed them as irrational. By doing so you filtered out any clues to a previous existence. But the fact that you are reading this book indicates that you are now considering the possibility of exploring your past lives; and you realize there may be issues in your present life that can only be fully understood by revealing a recurrent theme that links the present to the past. It is no coincidence that you are drawn to this subject. You are evidently ready to take the next step and discover who you really are.

If you answered 'yes' to between three and five questions, it indicates that you have intermittent and involuntary recall of a former life. You are ready to make a conscious connection with it, so that you can awaken these memories at will.

If you answered 'yes' to five or more questions, it suggests that you have an uncommonly strong connection with the Unconscious. You have the potential to develop spontaneous recall, which can reveal the pattern underlying a string of past lives and the purpose of your present incarnation.

HOW CAN I EXPLORE PAST LIVES?

The term 'regression' refers to techniques for recovering memories of past lives from the Unconscious mind. These techniques include guided meditations and visualizations; self-hypnosis; journaling, drawing and writing; dream interpretation; and using personal objects and photographs to trigger recall, among others. You can use these methods alone or work with a friend or a group. Though it is not essential, some people choose to consult a qualified regression therapist, a professional with the counselling training to provide guidance and help. All of these methods and options are explored in this book.

What will regression reveal?

Although the prospect of confronting unpleasant or disturbing memories from a former life may make you wary, there is nothing to fear or to feel anxious about. In most regression experiences, you are merely an observer of unfolding scenes and are more likely to find them intriguing than upsetting. You may also find them useful in offering insights into your present circumstances, personality and any recurring problems that you may have.

For instance, regression often offers clues to a current fear or phobia that has its origin in a past existence. Or you may discover the source of friction between you and another person that has troubled you since you met. On the rare occasions when you uncover something unpleasant, it is comparatively simple to assimilate the experience and achieve closure. When you do, you become a stronger, less fearful person for having confronted the issue.

You may also find that nightmares or a nagging anxiety have gone away.

How can regression help me?

It is a common misconception that you have to be suffering from a psychological problem to benefit from regression, and that all regression sessions are a form of therapy. On the contrary, the best reason for exploring former lives is to gain greater self-awareness.

Another fallacy is that memories of your past lives have been suppressed by the Unconscious mind because they are unpleasant. If this were true, you would only engage in regression to face your fears or to resolve past-life debts with other people.

In truth, one of the great benefits of regression is that it can help you to recover talents, skills and knowledge from neglected aspects of your psyche and empower you with the confidence to develop these gifts. Regression may help you reclaim your creativity or find your true vocation. It can also explain why you may feel unsettled in your present occupation and why you have an affinity for some activity or career you have been dreaming of since childhood. Regression can confirm that your intuition had been right all the time!

It can also help you to discover why you are attracted to a certain location and why you have an innate understanding of a subject, language or historical period that you have not formally studied.

Most significantly, perhaps, regression can offer answers to your questions concerning the meaning and purpose of life. It puts death into perspective, revealing it to be not the end, but a transitional stage between lives. Appreciating the natural cycle of life, death and rebirth lessens the pain of loss and takes the fear out of the unknown.

Things to remember

- Everything you have experienced in this life and all previous existences is accessible to you.

- Regression includes many safe and helpful ways of exploring past-life impressions.

- Your former lives can offer healing and empowering insights into current life circumstances.

Meditation and visualization

Meditation and visualization are time-honoured ways of quietening the mind to get in touch with the deeper layers of your consciousness. Once the busy mental chatter of everyday concerns has been stilled, past-life memories that may be stored in your Subconscious mind can begin to rise to conscious awareness.

Accessing the Unconscious

At some point you will undoubtedly want to explore the potential for recovering past-life memories on your own and at your own pace. Whatever technique you choose, you will need to be able to quieten your mind and withdraw into the inner world of the Unconscious, to replicate the light trance state that is attained under hypnosis.

Through meditation you can attain such a state within minutes, but it does take practice and patience to develop this ability. Setting aside time for meditation is still considered by many to be self-indulgent and even somewhat eccentric. Because Westerners are conditioned to believe that they must be constantly active and productive, you may also have to overcome your natural reluctance to sit quietly for 10–20 minutes.

The first step in overcoming this inner resistance is to stick to a regular routine, because once you have established the habit of meditating, you will find that it becomes pleasantly addictive. If you are new to meditation, be reassured that there is no need to feel anxious for any reason. You are *not* dabbling in the occult and you are not going anywhere – other than within yourself. And remember: you are in control at all times.

Contrary to popular belief, meditation is not the exclusive preserve of mystics or those who are 'spiritually advanced'. It is simply a state of being, in which you can still the restless chatter of the conscious mind so that you can hear the still, small voice of the Higher Self, which retains the impressions of every life it has lived.

How to quieten the mind

Meditation is the key to altered states of consciousness. Unless you master it, you will be dependent on others to regress you, so that you can connect with your past lives.

1   Close your eyes, immerse yourself in silence and don't anticipate having any visions or extraordinary experiences. Just enjoy the stillness. Sustain this blank canvas in your mind for as long and as effortlessly as possible.

2   If thoughts arise, note their passing, but attach no significance to them; bring your mind gently back to the focus of your meditation. You cannot control your thoughts, only your response to them. If you try to suppress them, you will attach significance to them and become distracted, with the result that your thoughts will control you.

Be patient with yourself and do not feel discouraged if you get distracted in the beginning.

3   When you are ready, open your eyes and return to waking consciousness.

4   It is likely that you will have found the exercise difficult – but be patient. You have been conditioned to believe that you must be active, and that relaxation is something you do in front of the television. Meditation is not the same as relaxation. It requires the body to be in a state of deep relaxation (as in sleep) and the mind to be in a heightened state of awareness.

Subjects for meditation

- **A still-life** Choose a simple object, such as a large pebble, a flower or an apple, and then lose yourself in contemplating its shape, texture and colour.

- **A family heirloom** For example, a watch or ring belonging to your grandparents.

- **Photographs of town and country life in the past** The earliest photographs date from the mid-nineteenth century.

- **A candle** Light the candle and, when you have fixed the flame in your mind, close your eyes and retain the image as long as you can.

- **An antique musical box** Ideal for connecting with the past and its previous owners, through psychometry (see page 52) and sound associations (see page 50).

Visualization

Also known as 'active imagination', this form of guided meditation has been a cornerstone of spiritual practice since ancient times. It is now an established technique used by psychiatrists and psychotherapists for exploring the symbolic landscape of the Unconscious and connecting with past lives. Although it involves the use of your imagination, it is different from idle daydreaming, in that the images are not consciously created by you, but arise spontaneously once you have set the scene. In effect, your imagination acts as the interface between the conscious and unconscious mind.

Unless you have a strong creative streak, you might consider your imagination to be redundant, or something to be wary of. However, it is the most powerful faculty you have for raising your awareness to other realities and attaining the altered states of consciousness that will allow you to regress.

Although you may find visualization difficult at first, it is essential to develop this skill, because its images and symbols are a direct and effective method of accessing past-life impressions. Once you have developed the ability to picture simple objects, and to sustain those images for five minutes or longer, you will find it comparatively easy to go deeper and allow such images to arise spontaneously. All you then have to do is explore the landscape. You will need to be able to distinguish a genuine past-life impression from one created by your imagination, but this becomes self-evident with practice and experience.

Easy visualization exercises

Try these simple visualizations until the images appear without effort and you can sustain them without any other images or thoughts intruding:

- A white dot on a blackboard.

- A number no greater than ten.

- A coloured balloon against a cloudless sky.

- A white feather or small white ball. See it rise with every in-breath and fall with every exhalation.

Once you can visualize these, you can elaborate by picturing the following:

- A white dot on a blackboard, which expands and contracts, then floats towards you until it is a size that you can step through. What do you see on the other side?

- A white feather or small white ball, which moves around the room with only your will to control it.

Creating a regression sanctuary

Having begun to meditate, you can encourage yourself to continue by creating a sacred space in a corner of your bedroom or study, complete with candles, crystals, incense, fresh flowers and inspirational pictures with a historical theme. Over time this 'regression sanctuary' will become 'charged' with your positive mental energy and a sense of peace, making it ideal for quiet contemplation.

Tips on making your own sanctuary

- Be selective in choosing your inspirational objects and pictures – clutter is *not* conducive to concentration.

- If you use candles, incense or oil burners, ensure that they are secure and that the room is well ventilated, because they consume oxygen and can cause headaches.

- Ensure your peace and privacy by putting a note on the door to the effect that no one is to disturb you. Take the phone off the hook, switch off your mobile phone and put on the answering machine.

- Try to avoid eating an hour before meditating, as it can be difficult to attain a sense of detachment if your body is busy digesting a heavy meal.

- Always record your experiences after each session in a journal (see page 46), because the images that arise may have a symbolic significance that you can analyse at a later date.

- If possible, try to find an antique chair that you can reserve exclusively for your time-travelling meditations. If you can afford it, there are plenty to be found at antique fairs; or perhaps you are lucky enough to have a friend or family member who has one to spare. Look for a carved wooden chair – the more unusual, the better. Wood is a natural accumulator of personal energy and will help you to tune into its history. A special chair will also have the psychological effect of promising a special experience every time you sit in it.

Regression-sanctuary relaxation routine

The more comfortable and relaxed you feel in your regression sanctuary, the more powerful and illuminating your past-life explorations will be. Here is a simple exercise to help you relax. You may wish to use this technique at the beginning of each session of regression work in your sanctuary.

1 Settle comfortably into your special chair, or whatever seating arrangement you have made (such as an inviting nest of cushions).

2 Allow your eyes to close gently. Bring to mind a place you have visited or can imagine, where you feel totally relaxed. Perhaps the place is a pleasant memory from a trip you have taken, or it might be an imaginary place where you feel totally safe. Breathe deeply in and out.

3 Imagine the place clearly, using all of your senses. Feel the warmth of the sun on your back as you lie on a tropical beach; smell the wood smoke of a cosy fireplace in a mountain cabin; hear the birdsong as you hike along a gentle forest trail.

4 As you continue to breathe deeply in and out, allow the feeling of relaxation that you associate with this place to fill your body, relaxing all your muscles – starting with your toes and moving slowly upwards to the top of your head.

5 Remind yourself that, as you explore your past lives, you are totally safe in your sanctuary, and affirm that everything you experience will enhance and heal your current life.

6 When you feel ready, begin to leave your special place and return to normal consciousness, without losing the sense of being totally relaxed.

This relaxed state is a good starting point for any of the regression meditations or visualizations you will learn in this chapter. It will also help you focus as you make notes in your past-life journal (see page 46) or read books about a period of history that you are exploring.

The Reincarnation Channel

Once you have established a strong connection with the Unconscious, you will be able to tune into your past lives as effortlessly as you change channels on your television. In fact, visualizing your past lives on an imaginary television screen is becoming an increasingly common regression technique.

You are in control

Watching your former self onscreen may sound like an episode from *The Twilight Zone*, but remember: the most direct method of connecting with the Unconscious is through the use of imagery. And because we have conditioned ourselves to feel relaxed in front of the television, this makes it an ideal method of regression. Another important benefit is that we feel in control of the television. And, as with real channels, if you don't like what you see on the Reincarnation Channel, you can always switch it off!

How to tune in

1 Sit in the chair you normally use to watch television. Close your eyes, focus on your breathing and visualize the screen in front of you. If you need help visualizing, simply open your eyes and fix the image of the television in your mind. As soon as you can sustain that image, visualize turning the television on and selecting channel 'R'.

2 Now visualize a small white dot in the centre of the screen. As you concentrate on the dot, it begins to grow larger – until it fills the screen. An image is forming. It is indistinct at first; the reception is a bit weak, as the set is still warming up. Can you adjust the tuning to get a sharper image?

3 There are a number of special features exclusive to this model: you can zoom in to examine details, or select slow motion and freeze-frame if you find something of particular interest. Best of all, you can enter a scene and re-experience a significant event from your past.

Grounding visualization

This exercise is a cornerstone of all meditation, and represents a vital element in past-life exploration. Unless you practise this simple visualization after every regression, you risk losing your sense of perspective. You might also experience a sense of light-headedness and lack of concentration that could have negative effects.

How to ground yourself

1 Sit in a chair with your back straight, your palms resting on your thighs and your feet flat on the floor. Take a deep breath, then relax into a steady rhythm, breathing in for a count of four, pausing for a count of two, then exhaling for a count of four.

2 When you feel relaxed, imagine that you are sitting with your back to a large, solid oak tree (or any other substantial tree). Feel the bark against your back; sense the strength of the tree supporting you, as a gentle breeze caresses your face and ruffles your hair.

3 Now sense a glow beginning to warm the soles of your feet. Visualize sending fibrous roots of etheric (psychic) energy into the soil to anchor yourself to the ground.

4 The warmth now rises through your lower legs into your thighs and on up into your back, reinvigorating your body with the universal life force and saturating every cell of your being.

5 As the warmth dissolves the tension in your back, you sense yourself merging with the trunk of the tree, becoming one with its strength and solidity. It has endured many storms through the centuries and will remain unshakeable for many more. Your anxieties dissolve and your sense of security is enhanced as you become aware of your connection to the earth and experience the shelter and protection of the tree.

6 Now return to waking consciousness by counting down from five to one. Open your eyes and stamp your feet once, to affirm your connection with the ground.

Opening the Third Eye

As we have seen, if you are serious about exploring your past lives on a long-term basis, you need to open yourself up to other levels of awareness through meditation and visualization, so that you can explore the Unconscious on your own whenever you wish to, without recourse to hypnotherapy. The key to attaining these altered states of consciousness is the process known as 'opening the Third Eye' – the organ of psychic sight.

How to feel the force of your aura

This exercise is the first stage in stimulating the Third Eye. Later on you will need to develop the facility for seeing with this inner eye, using visualization.

1 Close your eyes and establish a steady, natural rhythm of breathing.

2 When you feel suitably relaxed, bring the index finger of your right hand as close to the centre of your forehead as you can, without actually touching the skin.

3 Now take the finger away and bring it back again. Do this several times until you can feel resistance between the point of your finger and your forehead. This force represents the densest inner layer of your 'aura', or human energy field.

4 Once you can feel the elasticity of this force, begin to make small circles with the tip of your finger in the centre of your forehead. You should now sense a tingling or tickling sensation as the Third Eye is stimulated.

5 Visualize a sphere of white light in the centre of your forehead, and sense the warmth of its energy entering your Third Eye. See the white light in your mind expanding, until it envelops you. Now step into the light. What do you see on the other side? As you develop the faculty of inner vision, you will find that the Third Eye is stimulated involuntarily and the images become increasingly vivid.

The Garden of Memories

Here is a more advanced visualization exercise to help you access your past lives. Due to its length and the amount of detail it contains, it is useful to record the script. Remember to leave pauses at appropriate moments to allow you time to absorb the imagery and react with your inner guide. Alternatively, ask a friend to read the script while you relax. With practice you should be able to memorize sufficient detail to attempt the visualization without any reminders.

Exploring the garden

1 Make yourself comfortable in a chair, close your eyes and relax into a steady breathing rhythm.

2 Visualize yourself sitting in a cool, shaded room on a hot summer's day. Above you a ceiling fan is whirring – its soft, rhythmic, whooshing sound lulling you into a state of deep relaxation.

3 You are losing all sense of your surroundings and of the weight of your body in the chair. You are feeling detached, and as weightless as the curtains that billow in the breeze from the open window.

4 The next moment the curtains are drawn aside by the breeze, and the large french window opens, filling the room with light and the sound of a summer garden. The droning of bees and the melodic chirp of birdsong draw you outside, and you find yourself floating through the open window, as in a dream.

5 The scent of perfumed flowers is intoxicating. So too is the smell of freshly cut grass. The soft, sun-warmed breeze caresses your face as you emerge onto a balcony overlooking the garden and your eyes adjust to the glare.

6 There are ten steps leading down to the lawn and you are going to count each one, saying the following words as you descend: 'One ... going down ... two ... deeper ... three ... relax ... four ... down ... five ... going deeper ... six ... relax ... seven ... calm and centred ... eight ... feeling light ... nine ... all the way ... ten ... at peace.'

7 You can now feel the soft, springy grass under your feet. As you explore the garden, you become more and more content. You feel that you have come home to your personal sanctuary, on which the world cannot intrude.

8　Before you is an ivy-covered wall, and in the wall is a door leading to a sunken garden. You enter and find yourself again at the top of a short flight of steps. Count down as you go: 'One ... going down ... two ... deeper ... three ... relax ... four ... down ... five ... going deeper ... six ... relax ... seven ... calm and centred ... eight ... feeling light ... nine ... all the way ... ten ... at peace.'

9　At the bottom of the stairs you find a box of toys from your childhood, as pristine as the day you first played with them. Nothing has gone. Nothing is lost. Here there is no time.

10　Relive the pleasure you derived from play and imagination. Then move on to the centre of the garden, where you find a fountain, its waters bubbling and sparkling in the sun. You look into the water, but the reflected sun is dazzling.

11　For a moment you look away and, when you turn back, a shadow is cast over the water. It is the shadow of your inner guide, who now stands behind you. You look into the water and see its kindly face reflected. Then you turn and ask it the questions you need to have answered. And, when the moment feels right, ask it to reveal whichever past life is relevant to your present situation.

12　Your inner guide responds by gesturing to the fountain. You look into the water, and there you see your features change into those of your former self. Who were you? What are you wearing? What year is it? Look deeper into the water, and see images from the past appear from the depths. Feel free to ask questions and to request to see more.

13　When you are ready, the images will recede into the water and your guide will lead you gently back to the door of the sunken garden. Once there, retrace your steps to the house and, once inside, settle back into your chair and gradually return to waking consciousness.

Techniques for exploration

Past-life memories do not usually appear spontaneously, but need to be stimulated. You can use any or all of the safe and effective techniques described on the following pages – journaling, drawing, dreams, sounds and scents, psychometry, historical research and visiting historical sites, and pathworking – to explore your past lives. Each technique suggests different things to do and exercises to try, and you can safely use them on your own, without the help of a qualified regression therapist. Anything that stimulates your imagination is potentially useful, as long as you subject all recovered memories to rigorous scrutiny. However, when working on your own, choose a technique that makes you feel secure, rather than one that promises instant and impressive results.

A day trip to the past

Regression therapist Mandy Suter experienced her first connection with her past lives during a day trip to the English countryside and a visit to a castle of great historical significance.

'I have always intuitively known that there is more to us than the physical form, but I didn't have confirmation until I visited Arundel Castle. Although I had never been there before, I immediately felt as if I had come home. When I entered the Great Hall I went into a kind of dream state in which I saw medieval ladies in tall, pointed hats with veils and long sleeves, not as ghosts, but as glimpses into the past, as if they were part of the fabric of the building. I wasn't frightened, but excited. I felt that I belonged, but I also had the strongest feeling that my life there had been short. It wasn't a profound or life-transforming experience, but it was enough to confirm my beliefs in reincarnation. It also explained my lifelong fascination with tapestries, which I have been able to make, without ever having been taught.'

Drawing

Sometimes it is easier to tease out past-life impressions by drawing pictures and symbols, rather than using words, because imagery connects directly and more effectively with the Unconscious. Don't worry if you think you can't draw – this is *not* an art class.

Using imagery

For each of the following techniques, sit with a drawing pad and a pencil in your non-dominate hand (the hand you do not normally use for writing). You can use the images from a past-life regression as a starting point, or simply open yourself to impressions by following the instructions below.

Psychic art Relax by focussing on your breathing, and let your thoughts subside, leaving your mind as blank as

the pad of paper. Soften your gaze and allow yourself to be absorbed in the calming whiteness before you. You may see an image with your inner eye that appears to be in a space between you and the paper. Trace this before it fades. Then ask yourself pertinent questions to fill in more details regarding the place, period and significance of what you have drawn.

Doodling When you are suitably relaxed, ask your Higher Self to reveal memories of a past life that has relevance to the present. Let your hand move effortlessly across the paper, drawing whatever it wishes. Use the doodle as a form of note to be elaborated upon.

Figure from the past Draw the frame of a full-length mirror (it can be as simple or as elaborate as you wish). Within the frame draw the outline of a figure, without features or details of any kind. Next, focus on the clothes or facial features, and begin to sketch them in as if you were copying what you have seen in the mirror. When you have a detailed portrait of your past-life self, you can sketch in the surroundings, while probing your mind for a name, a year and any other details.

Journaling

Journaling is one of the most powerful tools you can use for self-exploration, because it requires you to process your thoughts and impressions before recording them in writing. These thoughts can then serve to catalyse subsequent inner journeys.

Feed your imagination

Initially you will find it useful to record the details of your regression sessions because the images can fade as swiftly as your dreams. However, once you have these clues to a past life, you can use them as triggers in a free association exercise to unearth more memories, or as the basis for factual research. They can also serve as prompts for further questions, which you can ask yourself in future regression sessions or during meditation. In addition, you can use your journal entries in the following exercises:

Dialoguing Recollect a character from a regression session or a significant dream, and then engage in a written dialogue. Write down the first thing that comes into your mind, regardless of whether it makes any sense to you at that moment. If you persevere with this dialoguing there will be a breakthrough, after which the words will flow from your pen before you consciously think of them. The resulting 'script' should be very revealing.

Clustering Begin by writing down in the centre of a page a significant detail from a past-life regression session, a visualization or a dream. Then draw a line to one edge of the paper and write the first word or phrase that comes to your mind. Circle it, then draw another line from this second bubble, and so on, until you have covered the whole page in circled clues and insights into your former lives.

Storytelling Select a dozen key words or phrases from a recent regression and link them in a story. Don't think too hard or analyse what you are writing. Simply allow the story to unfold and the characters to speak through you. You may discover that you have voiced subconscious concerns that link a past life to your present situation.

Write your own life story

This is a great exercise for oiling the wheels of your imagination – and it's fun. All you have to do is describe a day in your life as you imagine it to have been in a previous century. Choose a period for which you have an affinity, and a place which has always fascinatied you.

1   Describe your routine from morning to night, paying particular attention to your feelings, as well as to the detail of your surroundings: What did you do for a living? Who did you share your life with? What was your attitude towards them, and how did they treat you? Were there any distinctive features or unusual aspects of your life that you could verify using research resources, such as reference books, local archives or the Internet? What were the customs of your community?

2   Describe the prevailing atmosphere of the place and period. Were there tensions among your family or community? Was there anything special about the particular day that you found yourself describing? Did you recognize anyone in particular, or sense that they are with you in your present life for a specific reason?

3   Don't dismiss what you have written as fanciful. It might start off as such, as you draw upon obvious influences, such as what you have read and seen on television. But if you stick with it, your writing may surprise you, as you begin to tease out memories of a former life, one thread at a time.

4   Don't worry about grammar or spelling. The aim of this exercise is to get your creative cogs working. In fact, you may find that you begin to write in the distinctive vernacular of the period, and spell as you did in your former life.

5   Even if your initial effort appears to be pure fiction, it will serve as a valuable psychological exercise, giving insights into your personality, which you can then examine in regression or expand upon using a word-association exercise.

Dreams

The Austrian psychotherapist Sigmund Freud devoted his life to proving his theory that dreams are 'the royal road to the Unconscious'. And for the past century or so every branch of modern psychology has been founded on the belief that dreams are not mere fantasies, but a symbolic representation of our secret fears and desires. Dreams can also reveal a great deal about our past lives, which even hypnotic regression may be unable to draw out.

Reincarnational dreams

If you are going to work with your dreams, it is important to be able to distinguish between routine dreams (which are stimulated by what you have recently seen and heard) and those with a deeper significance. Past-life dreams (or 'reincarnational dreams', as they are sometimes called) are also often confused with lucid dreams, although they are in fact quite different.

In a lucid dream you suddenly realize that you are dreaming and are able to take control of the dream. But while lucid dreams give you the opportunity to explore the dream world and experience the exhilaration of flying and walking through solid objects, in a reincarnational dream you actually relive a past life, with all the emotions you had at the time. This makes it a much more powerful experience than one recalled in regression.

In a reincarnational dream you see everything from your own first-person perspective – you do not see yourself unless you look in a mirror or reflective surface. And you interact with other characters and move objects, just as you do in real life.

Another significant aspect of past-life dreams is that events occur in 'real time' and do not jump between scenes (as they do in fantasy). You experience an event as it occurred, although it may not be a significant event – merely one that you recall at random as typical of your former life. The danger with reincarnational dreams is that you have no control over which 'scene' you re-enter and, once there, you become the person you were in a former life. This can be upsetting if you are reliving a trauma. That said, if you are ready to deal with uncomfortable issues, you can clear your fears and phobias in one go, with no lasting ill-effects.

Things to remember

You can be sure that a dream is significant if you revisit the same period in subsequent dreams. Such episodes are known as 'serial dreams' and tend to recur until you identify the message they are trying to convey.

How to incubate a past-life dream scene

The main problem with dreamwork is that you cannot influence your dreams – or can you?

1 Before you go to sleep, choose a symbol that will act as a trigger when it appears in your dream. A clock or a door decorated with a question mark is an ideal image. Tell yourself that when you see this symbol in your sleep it will remind you that you are dreaming – and you can then take control of the dream. Repeat this instruction three times to imprint its significance on your Unconscious.

2 Now decide which period of history you wish to return to. Picture it as vividly as you can, but affirm in your own words that you will accept whatever experience is given for your guidance, insight and understanding. Affirm too that when you wake in the morning you will have full recollection of what you have dreamt.

3 Keep a journal and a pen by your bed, so that you can make notes the moment you wake, before the images fade.

Keeping a past-life dream journal

- A dream journal is a useful way of capturing past-life dreams.

- Keep your dream journal next to your bed, along with a pen.

- When you wake, lie in bed for a moment thinking about the dream you have had.

- When you feel ready, make notes about everything you remember, without elaborating on or censoring your account.

- Date your entry and delay reaching any conclusions, because related dreams may occur over a period of days or weeks.

Sounds and scents

If you have trouble visualizing, or if you find you are unable to enter a hypnotic state because you are constantly questioning and analysing the process, you may have more success working with your instinct, rather than your intellect. Two of the most effective techniques for triggering past-life recall are sound and scent.

Things to remember

- You will find a wide range of CDs and cassettes featuring natural sounds and ethnic instruments in gift shops and complementary health centres. Birdsong, the gently trickling waters of forest streams and the lapping waves of the ocean can be effective stimuli, as well as assisting relaxation.

- It is possible that you may have lived during the first half of the last century. If so, you could awaken memories of that time by listening to recordings of the radio shows and popular songs of the period.

- If, as is more likely, you lived in an earlier century, the traditional folk songs of a particular country or region may transport you to a specific place and period in history.

Music

Natural sounds and ambient music can be very effective in quietening the mind and helping you to shut out any distractions. Sacred chants and ethnic instruments can also trigger spontaneous past-life recall, because it is very likely that you will have lived at least one life in a tribal or devotional environment, and the distinctive sounds associated with these settings can serve as a shortcut to the Unconscious.

Striking a chord with the past

If you wish to experiment with the evocative power of music, follow the steps below.

1 Choose a song or instrumental passage that evokes a particular place, period or atmosphere for you.

2 Try to select something that does not have a connection with your present life or is associated with a film or television series, because this could confuse or unduly influence the imagery that you receive.

3 Make yourself comfortable, close your eyes and allow yourself to become lost in the music.

4 See if you resonate with an emotional chord that takes you back to a time in your life that is so vivid you can feel you are almost reliving it.

Scents as stimuli

In his autobiographical novel *Swann's Way* Marcel Proust describes a moment when he was transported back to his childhood simply by tasting a cake dipped in tea. In that moment, time ceased to have any meaning and his childhood was no longer merely a memory, but an alternative reality.

If you doubt that such a thing is possible, try rubbing an apple and inhaling the fragrance – see where it transports you. It is also worth experimenting with scented candles, incense and aromatic oils, which stimulate acute sensory cells in the brain, helping you to transcend time and space. You can use an electric diffuser to distribute scent into the air, or put a few drops of essential oil on your pillow before going to sleep to see if it stimulates a significant dream.

Experiment with the following fragrances and see what images they instinctively recall for you (as with all regression techniques, try not to have any preconceived ideas):

Rose A typical 'old-fashioned' fragrance that was popular with ladies in the Victorian and Edwardian eras. It might awaken memories of a former life in a country cottage or in a town house with a formal garden.

Lavender Has a soothing, therapeutic quality, and is used in aromatherapy for stress relief, headaches and insomnia. It is also valuable in clearing the mind prior to regression.

Eucalyptus Widely used as a decongestant, and a useful stimulant in regression because it is a very distinctive scent. If you suspect you might have had a past life in a Mediterranean country, this fragrance should create the right atmosphere for regression.

Lemon Has a refreshing, stimulating quality and is used to alleviate depression. Again, its unique fragrance makes it ideal as an aid to regression.

Psychometry

Psychometry is the ability to obtain visual impressions from a personal object such as a ring or watch – the theory being that we leave a residue of our energy in everything we have touched or worn. A psychic can pick up these impressions by tuning into the owner's unique vibration, and can describe details of their home and activities as if replaying a home movie. Psychometry is one of the most easily acquired psychic abilities, and yet its potential for use in past-life regression has not been widely explored.

Discover your family history

Imagine what you could learn about your family history simply by holding a ring belonging to your grandparents. Think what secrets you might uncover by selecting an item at random at an antiques fair. You can develop psychometry quite easily by practising the exercise below.

When you feel confident in your abilities, you will be able to tune into the past using objects belonging to friends and family. However, try to choose something belonging to someone whose details you can verify. Avoid using coins or other items that are likely to have been handled by many different people.

How to gain personal impressions

Ask a friend or family member for a personal item belonging to someone they know (or knew) well, so that they can verify the impressions you receive. The owner should wrap the object in a tissue or handkerchief so that it is not 'contaminated' by being handled by the intermediary.

1 When you receive the object, hold it between your thumb and forefinger. Then relax and quieten your mind.

2 Allow yourself to sink into a light trance state. Trust your intuition to bring images spontaneously to mind. Describe what you

see to the person who brought you the object, so that they can keep a record and check it with the item's owner.

Historical research

One effective, but controversial, method of exploring past lives involves reading to animate your imagination. Sceptics would argue that any memories recovered as a result of this are highly suspect, because they are almost certainly a recycling of facts and images obtained from the books. However, reading biographies, historical fiction and history books – as well as undertaking historical research and going to historical recreations – is as valid as any other conventional method, so long as you are aware of their potential to influence your regression experiences.

Using history as a lever

It is quite easy to test the validity of past-life memories recovered in this way. Simply keep a list of which books you have read or which research you have undertaken, and compare the notes made in your journal with the descriptions in the relevant source. At first you may find that you have merely embellished the scenes and characters, just as you incorporate everyday experiences into your dreams. However, in time the scenes described in these sources will serve as entrées to other levels of awareness, in the same way that snapshots and souvenirs can awaken forgotten images from the past.

And in virtually every country there are amateur groups dedicated to recreating the past by dressing up in period costume and living as their ancestors did for a day or a weekend. Although many of these groups concentrate on recreating battles, there are others with more peaceful themes. Again, you may not experience spontaneous recall in these situations, but you are likely to awaken memories that will later surface in your dreams. It should be relatively easy to distinguish between those that rerun your experience with the group and those that are genuine memories.

Triggering past-life recall

Reading and research can easily trigger past-life recall and stimulate past-life dreams. Spend some time learning about a time in history that particularly interests you: read historical novels, watch period films and study the pictures in illustrated books. Here are some questions to ask yourself. Note the answers in your journal:

- What is it about this period or event that intrigues me?
- What role would I want to have played in these events? Why?
- What connections can I draw between these events and my current life?

Visiting sites of historical interest

If you are going to explore your past lives without professional assistance, you need to find an 'aide-mémoire' – something that will help you establish a connection with the past – and visits to museums and historical sites frequently offer just such a tool.

Charge yourself with a site's energy

To tune into the site's atmosphere, simply choose an artefact for which you feel an affinity and stand as close to it as you can. You can keep your eyes open as you breathe steadily and enter a relaxed state of heightened awareness. Then close your eyes and see what impressions arise. The more often you practise this, the more sensitive you will become. You can then check your impressions with any facts displayed nearby, the guidebook, or perhaps with a curator who may be willing to share their knowledge (but don't admit your reason for wanting to know the history of the artefact, as they might not share your beliefs). The following ideas may prove useful:

Museum visits Although few museums allow visitors to handle the exhibits, some do. Even those museums that do not can still be useful for attuning yourself to the past. The atmosphere of such places is usually highly charged with personal energy from the objects' previous owners.

Working museums, cultural centres and pioneer villages Here you can see craftspeople practising traditional skills, which can be an effective visual aid to past-life recall. If they are modern recreations, you probably won't 'see' or sense anything of interest at the time, but your visit may well awaken memories that will surface later in your dreams.

Sites of historical interest Castles and old houses can be thick with atmosphere and frequently display an abundance of historical artefacts. Of particular interest are the homes of celebrated historical figures that make a point of preserving the interior as it was when the owner was alive, and which proudly display their personal possessions. Often it is the small domestic details and everyday objects that can trigger a recollection, rather than the setting itself. It is not necessary for you to have lived at this particular location in a former life to awaken memories of a previous existence, as long as the setting and furnishings are typical of the period.

Pathworking

Pathworking is a powerful ancient technique for exploring the symbolic landscape of the Unconscious. By meditating on the diagram known as the Tree of Life (see below) you can access specific aspects of your personality and discover how they relate to your past lives.

The wisdom of the Tree of Life

For example, if you suspect that you are too self-critical, you can explore the sphere on the Tree that corresponds to Judgement; this might reveal that in a former life you were conditioned by a domineering teacher, parent or partner to believe that nothing you did was good enough. If, however, you suspect that you let others take advantage of your good nature, you can explore the sphere of Mercy; there you can perhaps re-experience a past life in which you learnt that you were responsible for the well-being of others.

Things to remember

- Whichever aspect you wish to explore, you need first to enter the temple of the Earth, which serves to ground you, before moving on to the sphere of your choice.

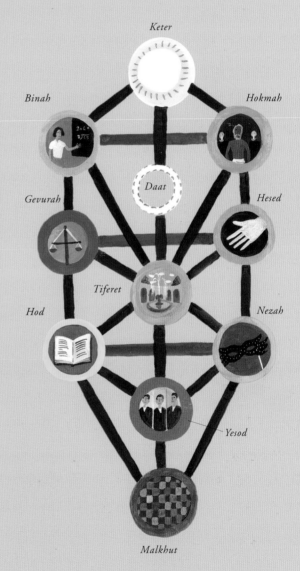

Keter

Binah   Hokmah

Daat

Gevurah   Hesed

Tiferet

Hod   Nezah

Yesod

Malkhut

Pathworking: the inner journey

Decide which aspect of your personality you wish to work on. Then familiarize yourself with the description of the corresponding scene symbolized by that sphere.

The Kingdom/Earth Contemplate this aspect if you need to be more practical and grounded. Visualize yourself in a small temple with a black-and-white chequered tiled floor, symbolizing the unity of opposites in the universe: male and female, active and passive, negative and positive. Ask the archetype of this level (the embodiment of certain human qualities to which we all aspire) to reveal the relevant life in which your sense of groundedness was undermined. Then you can clear the conditioning and recover this aspect of your personality. When you are ready, return to waking consciousness by counting slowly down from ten to one, then open your eyes.

Reverberation/Natural Intelligence Explore this aspect if you need be more receptive to new ideas or more decisive. The predominant colour of this chamber is yellow, the colour of the intellect. Visualize a study stocked with books and glass cabinets in which there are specimens of minerals, plants and chemicals. If you want to know why you sometimes find it difficult to make decisions without your emotions clouding the issue, ask the archetype of this level to reveal the relevant life in which this problem originated. You can also ask for the dissolving of emotional blockages accumulated in a former existence and the release of emotional attachments.

The Foundation/Self Contemplate this aspect if you have a tendency to undermine your own efforts or need to be seen to be right most of the time. This is the place to examine how you perceive the world and your self-image. Visualize a room of mirrors, or a tower with a window on the world below, where the predominant colour of the curtains and altar cloth is red, the colour of physical energy. Ask the archetype to reveal the relevant life in which your sense of self-worth was undermined, so that you recover your confidence.

Eternity/Instincts Explore this aspect when you need to get in touch with your sensual nature. The predominant colour of this chamber is orange, representing the emotions. A masked ball is taking place, which serves as an ideal setting to explore your attitude to pleasure. Meditating on this aspect can be particularly helpful if you need to know the source of guilt issues concerning your sexuality, or if you are acutely self-conscious. Accessing this aspect can restore courage, conviction and strength of purpose – qualities that may have been undermined by experiences in a former life.

Beauty/Higher Self Access this aspect when you seek perspective and guidance or need to overcome anger and resentment. Enter this chamber, which is furnished in green (the colour of harmony and regeneration) and is the inner sanctuary at the heart of the temple complex. Ask the archetype to reveal the reason behind recurring situations. Perhaps you have a karmic debt (see page 95) to resolve, or the Higher Self is creating situations that force you to question the wisdom of listening to the ego at the expense of your inner guide?

Judgement Contemplate this aspect when you need to be decisive. The dominant colour here is purple, the colour of insight and integrity. Appealing to the archetype may reveal that you suffered an injustice in a former life, which you can clear by choosing to forgive those who wronged you; or you may discover that you were too harsh on someone, to whom you can now make amends. Visualize a celestial court and consider the rules you have chosen to live under and enforce on yourself and others.

Mercy Contemplate this aspect if you need to practise tolerance and compassion, or believe you are too self-critical. The dominant colour of this chamber is violet, associated with transition and compromise. A court is the most suitable setting. Imagine yourself in the role of a defence counsel pleading mitigating circumstances in your own defence. Appealing to the archetype may reveal why you demand such a high standard from others and yourself. Identifying the root cause may help you to be less intense.

Understanding Explore this sphere when you are looking for insight into a particular problem. The dominant colour here is silver, representing contemplation and intuition. Visualize yourself confiding in a compassionate teacher, who graciously shares with you their knowledge and understanding of the world. Appealing to the archetype will reveal the significance of a difficult situation and how it relates to your actions in a former life.

Wisdom Contemplate this aspect if you seek to know why you hold certain opinions and beliefs. The dominant colour is gold, for revelation, which comes from considering the consequences of your actions. In practice this means that if you appeal to the archetype of this level, it will reveal the main theme underlying a series of your former lives and the karmic ripples that you have set in motion. Visualize yourself having a private audience with a guru or spiritual teacher in a setting that lends itself to quiet reflection.

THE ROOTS OF RELATIONSHIPS

Do connections between people recur over many lifetimes? Was your parent once your child? Have you and your partner been connected before, and are you *soul mates*? This chapter gives you the opportunity to explore the past-life roots of your current relationships. Doing so can give you insights into the hidden reasons for your connection and the deep causes of any problems – insights that you can use to improve your relationships.

Life's classmates

One theory about reincarnation holds that that there is no such thing as a 'chance meeting'. Every significant relationship has as its deeper purpose your soul's continuing education. If life is a classroom, important people in your life are like classmates – members of your *soul group*. While the same classmates may not appear in every lifetime, some do. Over lifetimes together, you have learnt many lessons with these soul companions.

Your relationship with a soul companion may be different from life to life. Parent and child, husband and wife, and even close friends may switch roles (in what is known as *role reversal*) and genders, or may even change from being a friend to being an enemy. You may continue to reincarnate with a significant other many times over many lives, until the lessons of the connection have been learnt and you both can move on.

Some theories say that a soul chooses the family into which it is born, to give it the perfect opportunity for growth and learning. Others hold that only highly evolved souls can choose their companions from life to life. For example, Tibetan Buddhists believe that a great teacher will incarnate in order to mentor the same group of students from life to life and continue their spiritual education.

Whether or not you believe that you have chosen your soul companions, if there are people in your life that you feel you have 'known for ever', then it's entirely possible that you have!

Have we known each other before?

A useful way to start this chapter is to use your journal to explore possible past-life connections with people with whom you have (or had) an unusually strong bond. Here are some prompts to start you thinking:

1. Make a list of people for whom you have had an especially strong positive or negative reaction – one that seems unwarranted by present-life circumstances. For each, can you imagine a different relationship; for instance, a friend may feel more like a sister, a child may be expert at 'mothering' you, or someone at work may feel like a jealous rival, though you cannot explain why. Make notes of what you've noticed, including any questions that arise.

2. What about each relationship would you like to understand better? How might understanding its past-life roots improve your current relationship? For example: 'I have always felt closer to Jan than to my own family. When I found out that I was

pregnant, I called Jan first. When we travelled to Florence together after college, we each had memories of having been there together before. My sister Susan has never liked Jan. Could Jan and I have been sisters living in Florence in a past life? If so, I could understand better why Susan doesn't like Jan. Maybe she's jealous of how close we were in the past.'

3. Keep your notes on hand and refer to them when you do the past-life exploration exercises included in this chapter.

Connecting with your soul group

Even though you may have a loving family and many close friends, there have probably been times when you felt as if you were travelling through life alone. But you are not. Each of us belongs to a group of like-minded souls that can be thought of as a form of extended family. Its members choose to reincarnate together in order to support each other and combine their collective experiences.

Recognizing your soul brother or sister

Although you may not be consciously aware of the existence of the other members of your soul group until you meet them, you are likely to feel a special closeness and empathy with them from the moment you connect. This is because they originate from the same aspect of the Divine Source and have a common purpose – the collective evolution of the group.

These individuals are likely to share your outlook on life, as well as your values and aspirations. They also have a disconcerting habit of appearing just at the right moment, as if in response to your call, whenever you need them. Some may be members of your own family, but each soul group is thought to contain dozens (perhaps hundreds) of individuals. So you may come together as friends, colleagues or as students and mentors. Occasionally your paths may cross so fortuitously that you dismiss the possibility of coincidence and consider the encounter to be fated. At other times the influence of your soul group may be more subtle. Each time the meeting will contribute to your understanding of your true place and purpose in life.

You think and act independently, but your sense of separation from the Divine Source is an illusion. When you connect with someone from your soul group, you will realize intuitively that they are an aspect of yourself. This intuition is accurate because soul-group members share an indivisible link in the collective consciousness we call God, or the Divine.

How to connect with your soul group

Connecting with your soul group is spiritual work of the most important kind. Fortunately, you do not need to do anything special to meet them. If you follow your intuition when you are offered opportunities to develop, learn new skills or contribute to the well-being of others, your soul group members will find you. However, you can assist the process by practising the following visualization.

1 Make yourself comfortable. Close your eyes and visualize a small sphere of white light in the centre of your forehead.

2 Visualize the sphere pulsating. At this point you might feel a tingling or tickling sensation, which confirms that you are stimulating your Third Eye (see page 41), the focal point of your psychic sight. You may even see a single eye looking back at you. This can be disconcerting at first, but remember that it is your own inner eye, which signifies a major breakthrough in your psychic awakening.

3 Focus the energy in the centre of your forehead and project the light into the outside world. There it will serve as a beacon for like-minded individuals who

have incarnated at this time, to help raise your awareness and find your true place and purpose in life.

4 Visualize yourself attracting these individuals into your life. Do not impose idealized features upon them, but keep them as vague figures so that you attract real people. See yourself learning from them, studying, working or simply discussing things with them.

5 Affirm in your own words that you are ready to meet your soul group and open up to its influence for your highest good.

6 When you are ready, return to waking consciousness by counting down slowly from ten to one and opening your eyes.

7 Do this visualization once a day for a week.

Using past-life memories to improve relationships

Your subconscious memories of past-life associations with people can shape your reactions to them this time around. The influencing memories can be either positive or negative. Perhaps the friend who always cheers you up when you're down has been doing so for many lifetimes. Conversely, a feeling of distrust for someone, which seems illogical, may be rooted in a betrayal that occurred in a previous lifetime.

The power to change

It is important to keep in mind that relationships are not 'fated' by your past-life connections. While past-life experiences may predispose you towards certain people and patterns in your relationships, past-life associations do not 'control' the people you meet or determine how you act and react. You are not 'fated' to marry your soul mate, or to fight with a past-life enemy in this life.

You always have the power to change your reactions and to transform difficult relationships into supportive ones. In fact, the opportunity to change past-life animosity into present-life love and compassion may be the reason why you have encountered a person again.

Using the present to reconcile the past

David was raised as an orthodox Jew and was determined to marry a girl who shared his background. When he met Carla, a German girl, he felt torn between appeasing his family, who distrusted anyone of German origin, and following his heart. Under regression, David recovered memories in which Carla's past-life family had persecuted David's German-Jewish family during the Second World War. In processing the images with the regression therapist, David came to understand that marrying Carla could help both sets of parents overcome their prejudices and preconceptions.

Exploring the past-life links of current relationships

You will need to devote at least half an hour to this exercise.

1 Choose a place where you will not be disturbed by anyone, and sit in a comfortable position. Close your eyes and take a few deep breaths.

2 Bring to mind a person in your current life with whom you have a strong bond, such as a parent, child, partner, friend or teacher. Picture this person vividly in your mind's eye. Include in your mental image details about the person's clothes, a particular place or setting, and what the person is saying or doing. Continue to build your mental picture until you have a strong sense of this person's presence.

3 Allow the details of this current image to dissolve, but retain the strong sense of this person's presence. Invite this sense of presence to reveal itself to you in a new setting, wearing different clothes and engaged in different activities. Tell yourself that you will recognize this person even if all familiar details are changed. Remain relaxed and explore the new scene that arises before you.

4 Now place yourself into this scene, making your mental image of yourself as vivid as possible. Imagine exactly what you are wearing. Imagine speaking to the person in question and hearing their response. Allow the scene between you to unfold in your mind's eye and see what happens.

5 When you feel you have learnt everything you can, stop the exercise, take a few deep breaths, open your eyes and return to normal awareness.

6 Write down everything that you remember in your journal as soon as possible. What did you learn about your present relationship from this possible past-life connection? Make notes about any insights that you received.

You can repeat this process many times to explore past-life memories of various people in your life, or to gain impressions of the lives you may have shared with someone. Once you start the process, new memories may surface spontaneously or in dreams. Keeping complete notes in your journal can help you make connections, see patterns and harvest insights.

Finding a past-life soul mate

Contrary to popular belief, it is not necessary (or even desirable) to connect with your soul mate during your present incarnation. Even if you were able to identify who that individual might be, you are more likely to learn from someone who will challenge you and complement your personality, rather than from someone who thinks and acts exactly as you do. If your present life is to have meaning and purpose, you need to learn the value of compromise, because it is only in the give and take of a dynamic relationship that true personal growth takes place.

What is a true soul mate?

If you do meet your soul mate and feel that you cannot live without them, this does not necessarily mean that you should give up everything for them. There might be another purpose for your meeting. Many relationships have been wrecked because an irresponsible psychic or fortune teller persuaded an individual they should leave their present partner for someone who had been their soul mate in another incarnation. In such circumstances it is surprising how even the most intelligent and well-balanced individual can let their heart rule their head, if they believe their actions have been pre-ordained and endorsed by a higher power. Often they persuade themselves that the person they desire is 'meant for them' and that their illicit relationship is karma – destiny – as if it had been decreed and they are obliged to obey. However, this is to miss the true meaning of what a soul mate is.

A soul mate is *not* a refuge from reality, or someone provided by Providence to make you feel good about yourself, even when you are wrong. The true soul mate is someone with whom you share the experience of life in all its variety: good, bad and indifferent. You will know you are with them when you do not have to explain yourself, because they understand implicitly how you feel. In their presence you will feel secure and share an understanding that will not necessarily involve romantic love or physical attraction.

That is not to say that seeking out your soul mate is an unnecessary diversion. Such people can provide crucial support. But if you make your search for a soul mate the focal point of your life, you are likely to miss opportunities that are provided for your advancement. There is also a serious risk that you may be tempted to use your search for a soul mate as an excuse to avoid commitment. And it is only through commitment that you give yourself and your prospective partner a chance to become fully realized and responsible human beings.

Things to remember

- It is often assumed that a soul mate is always of the opposite sex and is destined to be your lover.

- Your soul mate can, however, be your best friend, or even a parent or child with whom you will journey through a significant incarnation.

The myth of twin souls

Do not confuse soul mates with 'twin souls', which are derived from the New Age movement. In contrast to soul mates, who are mutually compatible individuals sharing a similar spiritual path, twin souls are supposedly divided at their moment of creation and incarnate separately, but are fated to meet and find fulfilment; without their ideal other half, they are incomplete. Of course we are all complete individuals and are not dependent upon anyone else to fulfil our divine potential. Even if it were possible for a single soul to split in two, surely each would still be a unique individual (just like physical twins)?

Encounter in Egypt

Would you recognize your soul mate if you met them by chance? The following true story suggests that you would. Barbara Jaeger went to a meditation meeting and immediately felt a connection with the lady who was teaching the class.

'At first I couldn't remember where I had known her, then I was certain that we had been together in an earlier time. She picked up on this and asked me to close my eyes, let my mind go blank and see if I could recall more details. Immediately I saw the two of us cowering in the corner of a huge temple in ancient Egypt. Before us stood a tall man covered in glistening red-ochre body make-up. He wore a headdress with the head of a cobra

and an amulet embossed with a serpent. There was a broad scar running from his wrist to his elbow, and a piece was missing from his left ear.

'I was not observing this – I was experiencing it again. Even though we were sitting in a draughty hall in England in midwinter, I was sweating profusely as if I were physically back in the baking heat of Egypt. But the most remarkable aspect was the fact that when I came out of the trance, the teacher told us that she had described the very same scene during a recent regression. She was able to fill in the missing details and put the scene in context, whereas I had only had a fleeting glimpse.

'Even after such a remarkably vivid vision I needed to know that what I had seen had been real, so the next day I went to the library to research the period. I pulled out a book on ancient Egypt and opened it at random. There before me was a picture of the amulet with the serpent. I must admit I dropped the book in shock.'

How to find a past-life soul mate

Keeping in mind the cautions described earlier, if you do wish to find a soul mate, here is a technique you can use. It is based on the ancient art of scrying: seeing an image in a crystal ball, a bowl of water or, in this case, a mirror.

1   Choose a good-quality mirror. Make sure the surface is clean.

2   Place the mirror slightly above you, so that you are not gazing at yourself when you look into it. Position it so that it reflects nothing but a blank wall. You may wish to darken the room and place candles on either side of the mirror for light.

3   Gaze into the mirror. After a few minutes the surface will begin to appear milky, almost as if the mirror were covered with a fine mist or white fog. There is no need to strain to concentrate. Simply hold in your mind the intention that an image of a soul mate from a previous lifetime will appear in the mirror.

4   Affirm to yourself that seeing this person will cause no harm to your present relationships. Rather, viewing the image of a soul mate will comfort you with the knowledge that you have enjoyed many significant relationships in your past lives and will enjoy many more.

5   Keep gazing at the mirror until an impression of a person forms. Some people may see unfolding in the mirror a whole scene with this person; others may simply catch a brief glimpse.

6   Whatever you see, you are satisfied and happy about it. When the image clouds over or fades, take a few deep breaths and thank your inner guide for its help.

7   Write down whatever you remember in your journal, knowing that you can use the mirror to gather more details whenever you like.

Children's past lives

It is not unusual for young children to refer to a former life in a candid, matter-of-fact manner that can catch their parents off-guard. The best way to respond to such casual revelations is to be equally objective, and to ask for more details as naturally as you would ask what they want for lunch. In this way children see that you are taking them seriously and accept the idea as perfectly normal. At the same time you do not reveal yourself to be over-eager to be told a sensational story – real or otherwise. If children are merely fantasizing, you are more likely to establish this by teasing out subsequent details in the course of conversation than by confronting them with a direct question, which simply implies that you don't trust them to tell you the truth.

Reliving the First World War

From an early age Martin exhibited a deep distrust of adults, and even of other children, which puzzled his parents. At school he kept his distance from his classmates and would often describe scenes of death and destruction with a self-conscious giggle, which a child psychologist diagnosed as a symptom of an underlying anxiety.

Then one day, at the age of seven, Martin casually declared to his astonished parents that he had been a German child during the First World War and that he had been murdered by British soldiers. He was able to give them a surname, the year and the name of the town. His parents were convinced that Martin was not trying to impress them with a lurid fantasy, because they had never shown him any films or documentaries of the period and he had no interest in that era or in wars of any kind.

Fortunately Martin's parents took their son's story seriously. After they had explained to him that such horrors are extremely rare, and reassured him that the past would not repeat itself, the child became less fearful, more sociable and an enthusiastic pupil.

Exploring the past lives of your children

Because children so readily remember their past lives, you can often pick up past-life clues from their behaviour, including clues that point to any previous connection with you. Here are some things to look out for:

- **Children often talk spontaneously about their past lives** If your child calls someone in the family by an unusual name – one that the child seems to have made up – this name might be a clue to a past-life. For instance, a girl might call her brother 'James' even though her brother's name is 'John' because she had a brother called 'James' in a previous life.

- **Unusual talents may also be a clue to a child's past life** A child with a past life as a musician might be able to repeat a song heard only once, or pick out melodies on the piano.

- **Children's imaginary games can also provide past-life clues** One boy's favourite game was 'rescuing children from a burning building'. This game might be a clue that the boy had died in a fire with his children in a previous lifetime and was determined to escape safely this time.

Perhaps the most intriguing possibility is that your child is the reincarnation of a deceased family member. Sometimes a child might remember people who were close to the deceased relative – even people they have never met. One young boy, when visiting his grandmother, pointed to a photograph of his dead grandfather's brother (a man who had died long before the boy was born) and said, 'That's Thomas', which was indeed his great-uncle's name. From this clue and others, it seemed that the boy might be a reincarnation of his own grandfather!

Role reversal

Until the age of five, when children lose their connection with the upper worlds, it is not uncommon for them to act like 'old souls' trapped in children's bodies. They may demonstrate unusual talents, or behave like little adults, particularly towards their younger brothers and sisters. Often they are merely imitating their parents, but such attitudes can indicate that memories of a former life are just below the surface and could be teased out by means of tactful questions.

Father and son

Four-year-old Jordan and his father, George, had never really connected. Jordan showed little affection for his father and even appeared to resent his presence, although George (a single parent) had raised him devotedly and made a great effort to please the boy.

George became desperate, as he felt he was missing the most precious years of their relationship, so he consulted a reputable psychic. The reading revealed that Jordan had been George's father in a former life, and that the boy now resented being dependent on George, because their previous relationship had ended in the same way. In their past life Jordan had become terminally ill in old age and had to rely on his son to feed, bathe and attend to him. This deprived him of his self-respect and left him feeling indebted to his son. The psychic was able to read the child's character just by looking at him, and tell George that Jordan did not share his father's need for demonstrative displays of affection and reassurance.

After the reading George was more patient with his son and would talk to him as an adult, making an effort to show that he valued the child's opinion. He explained that he enjoyed caring for his son and did not do it out of a sense of duty. In time their relationship improved and they became very close.

Watching for clues

Role reversal is a comparatively obscure aspect of the past-life experience, but one that can offer significant clues into the dynamics of family relationships, particularly between a child and its parents.

If your child, or a member of your family, has exhibited a maturity beyond their years, it is possible they might have been a member of the family in a former life. If you are the parent of a child who occasionally refers to members of the family who died before they were born, you can test the validity of these 'memories' by engaging in role-play using their dolls. Ask the child to imagine the dolls visiting a house where they used to live, and make a note of

the names they use and the roles they assign to the dolls. However, make sure you do not to use any leading questions, and end the exercise if the child becomes uncomfortable or loses interest.

Have you experienced role reversal?

To explore the possibility that you might have been the parent to your mother or father in a former existence, find a quiet moment when you can be certain of being alone. Then ask yourself the following questions.

1 Do you intuitively treat one of your parents or an older member of the family as if they were your younger brother or sister?

2 Do you share confidences with them as you would with a younger sibling? Do you feel protective towards them, despite the fact that they are older than you?

3 Can you recall incidents when you acted as the more responsible member of the family?

4 Did you ever resent being treated as a child, and do you still feel uncomfortable in your role within the family?

5 When you were young, did you exhibit adult behaviour and express ideas that seemed at odds with your age (unlike a precocious child, who merely imitates adult behaviour)?

6 Did you recall people and specific events with which your grandparents would have been familiar, or use archaic expressions peculiar to a particular period? (You may need to ask your family to confirm these suspicions).

PAST LIVES AND PRESENT HEALTH

Today many people accept that some *physical symptoms* are trying to give us a message. For example, back or shoulder pain may indicate that you are trying to bear a responsibility that is too heavy. Past-life exploration adds a new dimension to interpreting your symptoms, as the causes of current health problems can sometimes be traced back to an event that happened in a previous life.

Past-life links to current ailments

Chronic or recurring illnesses are especially suggestive of past-life links. You may enter a current lifetime with a predisposition to problems in a particular part of your body. For instance, problems with your throat or chronic hoarseness may indicate that something prevented you from speaking up for yourself in a previous lifetime. Addictions and other emotional conditions may also have past-life causes. Smoking, eating disorders, phobias, sleep disorders and sexual problems often have their roots in past-life experiences.

The techniques in this chapter provide tools that you can use to explore the connections between any current health problems and your past lives. Use your journal to investigate any troubling condition. If you have migraines, write down when they occur, describe what you experience and make note of any unusual thoughts or dreams that accompany them. If you are addicted to smoking, note how you feel when you reach for a cigarette and any associations that you

have with tobacco, smoke, fire or matches. Use active imagination to explore past-life associations with your condition or addiction. You may be surprised by what you discover.

Understanding the deep causes of your current symptoms and emotional problems may not cure them. However, today even conventional medicine recognizes that meditation, guided imagery and other mind-body techniques can contribute to the healing process. Insight into the past-life causes of current problems can help to relieve your anxiety; feeling more relaxed and at peace can help you cope better with your condition. It also releases stuck energy, which can strengthen your immune system, activate your body's defences and help you to heal.

Physical symptoms as clues

If you have a chronic physical complaint you must consult a medical professional. However, if they can find no physical or emotional source, you may have to look for clues to your ailment in a former life. Below is a list of some of the more common psychosomatic disorders and possible past-life causes. Once you have identified which (if any) of these might be applicable to your own condition, you can work towards a cure with a regression therapist or bodywork specialist to erase the imprinted memory and release the pressure.

The cause of your ailments

Head Migraines can be symptomatic of an unwillingness to acknowledge an unpleasant experience, or a reaction to some kind of pressure.

Eyes Recurrent eye infections and psychosomatic glaucoma may be symptomatic of problems of perception. You might have witnessed something so horrific in a former life that you have willed yourself to be blind to injustice or brutality in the next life.

Ears Recurrent ear infections and a reluctance to react when other people talk to you can indicate an unconscious desire to ignore what you do not want to acknowledge. You are effectively 'turning a deaf ear' to the facts that may have originated in a former life, when perhaps you were falsely accused of something such as heresy or witchcraft.

Mouth Persistent mouth ulcers and a dry mouth when you are trying to speak suggest problems in a past life with self-esteem and self-expression. In extreme cases these can be self-inflicted, to atone for having falsely accused someone in a former life.

Nose and throat Sinus problems and persistent sore throats may be indicative of a death by drowning, suffocation or strangulation.

Neck, shoulders and back Aches and pains in these areas can indicate a reluctance to bear a burden or more than your share of responsibility. The most

common source is a former life in which you had to raise a family by yourself.

Stomach Digestive disorders can be attributed to suppressed emotions, such as bitterness, resentment and anger. In the most serious cases this 'dis-ease' of the soul manifests as cancer in the physical body, as the unprocessed emotional energy poisons the body's cells.

Skin The most common form of skin complaint is eczema, which may be symptomatic of the need to 'get out of your skin' – either because you are uncomfortable being yourself or because you feel acutely vulnerable. An experienced therapist will be able to identify whether the source of the problem lies in the present or the past.

Genitals Impotence, frigidity and lack of bladder control could be attributable to the guilt or fear created by a trauma such as rape in a past life (see sexual dysfunction on page 87).

Legs and feet Stiffness, swollen ankles, leg ulcers and other ailments of the lower limbs are likely to be manifestations of the need to escape and run away, conflicting with the knowledge that this is impractical or impossible. If the source does not originate in the present, it may be traced back to a former life when you were imprisoned or denied the opportunity to leave your home because you had commitments or obligations.

Hands Arthritis and clumsiness may manifest to express a fear of being unable to hold on to something of value. In a previous life you may have suffered a traumatic bereavement, such as the loss of a child, enforced separation or loss of status, self-respect or precious possessions.

War wounds

Philip was plagued by stomach disorders throughout his adult life, yet his doctor could find no physical cause for his debilitating complaint. Under regression it transpired that he had been a soldier during the First World War and had suffered from shell shock, which had left him acutely anxious and afflicted with stomach cramps. Denied the chance of a discharge on medical grounds by an unsympathetic army doctor, Philip was sent back to the front and was fatally wounded by a bayonet in the stomach, which led to a slow and painful death.

Psychic artist Sylvia Gainsford, illustrator of *The Tarot of the Old Path* and *The Kabbalah Cards*, was haunted by a recurring dream in her childhood, which appears to have been a clue to a former life. 'In the dream I was in the midst of a terrible battle. It was fierce hand-to-hand combat and I was so frightened that I fled the field. It was so vivid and real, it wasn't like a dream at all. I remember being afraid for my life and running until I couldn't run any longer. Then I stumbled and fell. I lay still for a while, hoping that the enemy would walk by thinking I was dead, but the next moment I was shot in the back and awoke in a cold sweat, with a real pain where the bullet had entered. It took a few moments for that feeling to fade. Later in life I had serious kidney problems; this is where the bullet would have lodged, and I have always believed it was guilt that brought this on. I was punishing myself for having abandoned my comrades.'

Discovering a symptom's past-life cause

If you think that a particular symptom from which you are suffering may be rooted in the past, try this exercise to discover the past-life connection.

1   Begin by scanning your body for tension in every muscle and joint, from your forehead to your toes. As you work your way down your body, tighten each muscle and hold it clenched for five seconds before releasing. This process consciously acknowledges the tension that is present, even when you think you are relaxed.

2   Now repeat this affirmation to yourself three times: 'I am now in a state of deep relaxation and becoming acutely aware of the subtle influences that have manifested as [name the symptom you are suffering from]. Does this dis-ease originate in a past life and, if so, what were the circumstances that created it?'

3   Allow the images to arise spontaneously. You may relive a scene from that life, or see a colour relating to a specific chakra (or energy centre, see page 89) in the subtle or etheric body. If so, visualize a radiant sphere in that colour hovering over the affected area, and then absorb it into your body. Sense the heat dissolving the blockage, dispelling the dark matter of infected tissue and regenerating the cells.

4   Alternatively, you may ease the problem simply by performing the exercise, because you have shown a willingness to clear whatever caused it. Often the discomfort is the result of an unwillingness to let go of something or someone from your past, and the accumulation of fear or guilt over the intervening years.

5   What sensations do you associate with that part of your body? Do not be surprised if you are drawn to an area that you have not previously associated with pain. Follow the chain of associated images in your mind – no matter how surreal or unrelated they appear to be. The connection will be made plain, and you will be able to identify and clear with ease the source of your dis-ease, simply by affirming your willingness to let go of your past life or to forgive yourself or another person associated with that period.

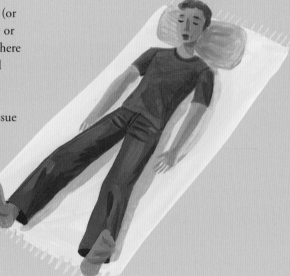

Bodywork

Bodywork is a method of retrieving past-life impressions by working on a specific area of the body where a memory may be stored. If, for example, you were fatally injured in a former life, it is likely that a resonance will have been left on your subtle body (see page 89); this can be released by manipulating the corresponding part of your anatomy. Emotional problems from a past life can also leave an imprint on the subtle body or restrict the free flow of energy, manifesting as chronic ailments in your present life.

Different bodywork techniques

Such issues need to be addressed using a suitable bodywork technique, such as shiatsu, reflexology, osteopathy or acupressure, because they are rarely cured by conventional medicine. If you suspect that your symptoms have a psychosomatic origin, you may find kinesiology effective – it measures how your muscles react to specific stimuli and it is particularly suitable for identifying regression issues.

All forms of holistic healing put clients into a deep state of relaxation, during which they are receptive to impressions from the Unconscious and are able to release repressed emotions. So it is not uncommon to experience spontaneous past-life recall during complementary therapies such as reiki, shiatsu and reflexology. If a bodywork session does trigger a strong memory that seems to be linked to a past life, take everything you experience as a piece of the puzzle and, if you do not feel comfortable discussing it with your bodywork therapist, consult an experienced regression therapist.

Be prepared for the unexpected

Brian's experience of bodywork is typical: 'I was having healing as part of the reiki initiation process and had gone deeper into relaxation than usual, when suddenly I had a vision of a family sharing a meal in ancient China. I observed the scene through the eyes of what I believe was my former self, seated at one end of a long, low table. At the other end was a woman whom I instinctively "knew" was my mother, both in that life and in my present incarnation. I didn't get any verifiable facts, but it was still a significant experience, as I now feel a stronger link with my mother and a sense of responsibility for her welfare, for I believe we are spiritually linked for our mutual benefit.'

Past lives and current emotions

It is now generally accepted among orthodox medical practitioners that many chronic ailments are psychological or emotional in origin. In most cases, this dis-order or dis-ease is the physical manifestation of unresolved issues originating in the patient's recent past, but in a small percentage of cases the source of the problem might lie even further back – in a former life.

Balancing the physical and emotional bodies

Our feelings can have a profound and lasting effect on our health and well-being, as we have both a physical and an emotional body, each of these being dependent on the other. Unresolved conflicts, particularly those involving an intimate relationship, can seriously affect the balance between the two. The more intimate the relationship, the stronger the resonance it will leave, or the imprint on the matrix of etheric energy that makes up our emotional body (also known as the subtle or dream body).

If this relationship was distressing or destructive, then the resulting vibrational disturbances can disrupt the flow of etheric energy through the body, resulting in ill health or psychological disorders in a former life and the next. After a traumatic experience the mind automatically suppresses any seriously unpleasant memories, and we usually need professional help to identity, address and process

these images and their associated feelings. But if we die with these issues unresolved, they can carry through into the next life.

If you are currently suffering from anxiety, fears, phobias, a lack of confidence, inexplicable outbursts of anger, jealousy, resentment or regret, and you cannot trace the cause to an incident in your recent past, then the answer may lie buried deep in your unconscious. In that case you need to work through the regression exercises on the following pages and be prepared to release repressed emotions, if they surface.

Eating disorders

Anorexia and bulimia are generally thought to be symptomatic of emotional problems, specifically a lack of self-worth. However, in rare cases these two very modern disorders may be a manifestation of a deeper dis-ease that originates in an earlier incarnation. If you experienced rejection in a former life by a parent, partner or lover, then the emotional impact of that abandonment may echo down the ages and manifest in a desire to literally waste away, so that you are not a burden to anyone.

Obesity, too, can originate from a traumatic experience in a former existence. During regression some obese people revisit their death by malnutrition, when their last thoughts were that they would never again allow themselves to starve to death. Often it is such slow, lingering deaths (rather than a sudden violent end) that imprint themselves on the subtle body and determine our behaviour over several lifetimes.

Addictions

Whether the object of gratification is drugs, alcohol, sex, shopping, power, food or fast cars, the underlying cause of most addictions is invariably psychological rather than biological. And in many cases the source of addiction is not in this life, but in the last. For example, if you died in poverty, you might reincarnate with an all-consuming passion for money and possessions in order to insulate yourself against privation or to prove to yourself and the world that you have overcome adversity this time around.

In several cases regression has been used to trace a client's alcohol addiction to a former life in which they died during surgery on the battlefield, where alcohol would have been used as a crude form of anaesthetic. In such cases their final thoughts usually were 'There won't be enough for me' – and this fear carried through into their next incarnation. Others, who had seen more suffering than they could endure and who feared that they

might be forced to experience more in their next life, were driven to seek escape from reality in either alcohol or drugs. However, once this compulsion was revealed to them through regression, they were able to seek treatment for their anxiety and subsequently lost their craving.

You can also be emotionally addicted. Many people find themselves drawn to the same type of partner because they cannot break the cycle of addictive behaviour learnt in previous lives. Those who are fixated with playing the role of rescuer may discover that they were a domineering parent in a former life and did not allow their children to learn from their own mistakes. Unless they correct this trait, their prospective partner will learn to exploit the situation and eventually they will separate.

Conversely, those who did not learn to assert themselves in a previous life may find that they endure the role of victim, and suffer emotional or physical abuse, because it serves to endorse their belief that all men (or women) are bad and they are not worthy of genuine affection or consideration.

Depression

Although depression can usually be traced back to a specific source, it is now recognized that certain individuals feel a deep melancholy without any identifiable cause for their condition. Seasonal

Affective Disorder (or SAD), to give it its clinical term, is thought to be due to a chemical imbalance in the brain associated with a change in the seasons. However, in some cases there may be a link to a deep-seated memory from a former life.

If in a past life you suffered a traumatic loss, or endured an extremely unpleasant experience, then you may succumb to a vague sense of helplessness

and despondency at the relevant time of the year. Certain locations or events can also trigger indefinable feelings of sadness, fear or unease, if there is an unconscious connection with an event in a former life.

Insecurity and anxiety

Insecurity takes many forms, but one of the most common is a fear of commitment. If in a past life you died abandoned or alone, you might be reborn with a voracious appetite for affection. This could impel you to seek reassurance in short-term relationships that would insure you against the prospect of disappointment.

If, however, you were a grief-stricken parent whose children died in infancy from a lack of food, medicine or shelter (a not uncommon occurrence in previous centuries), you might be reborn with a deeply ingrained belief that there will never be

The tears of the clown

As a boy, Trevor refused all efforts from his parents to take him to the circus. He said that the clowns made him feel sad. As a young man he underwent regression and discovered that, in a former life, he had been taken to the circus by his father in an attempt to cheer him up in the final days of a fatal illness – that is why the laughter of the crowd now seemed hollow to him.

Years later, when he had a son of his own, Trevor inexplicably lost this sad association. During a psychic reading he learnt that his son had been his father in his former life and, now that they were reunited, the pain of separation had been healed.

enough of whatever you need in order to feel secure. Again, you would probably be unaware of the reason for your anxiety, but regression or a psychic reading might reveal a specific incident in a past life as the source of your insecurity. This is usually sufficient to clear the anxiety; if not, it can be addressed by a short course of hypnotherapy.

Phobias

Fear is a natural human response to danger – a critical element of our survival instinct – whereas a phobia involves an irrational fear of something that does not present an immediate or real danger to the person who is affected by it. In most cases the object of their fear is symbolic of a general insecurity, a vague anxiety concerning the future and their own mortality.

However, in some cases the focus of their fear represents something connected with an event in their past, which has been suppressed to such an extent that the sufferer does not recall what it is they are actually afraid of. Instead, they unconsciously substitute something that it is socially acceptable to be afraid of, such as spiders, snakes or enclosed spaces. In rare cases a phobia is rooted in a traumatic event in a former life, of which the sufferer may be unaware and thus unable to clear without professional help.

A fear of water

Writer Howard Rodway, author of *The Psychic Directory*, used to have an inexplicable fear of still water. 'I couldn't walk near a pond or lake without breaking into a cold sweat,' he recalls. 'It might sound odd, but it was a serious phobia. Then I met a medium who said she knew that I had a fear of water – and the reason why. I hadn't mentioned it, so naturally I was intrigued. She said that in a former life I had been murdered by drowning. Immediately I felt that what she said was true, and my fear began to subside. A year or so later I wrote to her in connection with the directory I was compiling, and she picked up more details just by handling my letter. She was able to tell me that I had been a Dutch farmer with a ranch in Quebec, Canada, and that I had been married to a half-Cherokee girl called Kitty. We had been murdered by our enemies and dumped in a lake. The queerest part is that, unbeknown to the psychic, my first wife in my present incarnation was also a half-Cherokee, which suggests that we hadn't completed our life together the first time round.'

The emotional journey

Ideally you should perform this exercise while lying down on a bed or mat, with a small pillow supporting your neck. Although it may seem simple, this exercise has the potential to awaken strong feelings and suppressed memories, so do not attempt it if you have suffered a recent trauma, or if you believe that you may not be able to deal with your feelings without professional help. You may wish to work with a trusted friend, who could use the following script to guide you and record your response. A friend would also be helpful in offering moral support and reassurance, should you become uneasy. Remember: you are in control and can end the session at any time, by counting down slowly from ten to one and opening your eyes.

1 When you feel suitably relaxed and your mind is still, think of one word to describe the way you feel at this moment. Accept the first word that comes to mind. Perhaps you feel anxious or excited at the prospect of what you might discover during this journey; have a nagging doubt about whether it is possible to probe into past lives at all; or feel there is an emotional 'theme' to your life, such as insecurity or frustrated ambition, which you can now take the opportunity to explore.

2 Focus on that feeling. Indulge it for a moment and see where it takes you. If there is excitement or anxiety, does it originate in your head or your solar plexus? Is it a feeling you can follow to the source, or a mental safeguard you have created to protect yourself until you are ready to process the past? Trust your intuition to give you the answer. If you doubt the possibility that you can explore past lives, could this be a self-defence mechanism to prevent you from doing

so until you have reached the necessary level of understanding and awareness? Again, trust your intuition to lead you on through imagery that you can explore.

3 See if you can locate the source of those feelings by visually scanning your body. You may, for example, be uncomfortable or acutely self-conscious when exploring your feelings. But by probing in this way you may discover that it is because in a former life you were made to feel inferior or effeminate (if you were a man) for doing so, by a domineering parent or adult. You may have a fear of violence or disease, or a phobia of heights or confined spaces. All of these can originate in a past life, and you can identify their source by following the feeling associated with a part of the body. For instance, if you trace the fear of violence, you may discover that you become blocked in one particular part of your body, and that by focussing on it you stimulate images of a past life in which you suffered a fatal wound there.

4 By following your feelings you will awaken imagery associated with that feeling, meeting people with whom you can interact or a specific scene that you can explore. For example, you may be acutely self-conscious in a social situation, or distrustful of people in general, for no reason that you are aware of. By exploring your feelings you may discover that in a former life you were persecuted for your beliefs or you were the victim of an injustice.

5 Alternatively, you may be drawn to an area of darkness. Do not be apprehensive – this is a fear that needs to be identified and experienced, so that it can be cleared. You are quite safe. This is a mental and emotional journey, not a physical one. You cannot be harmed in any way, and you will not feel anything. Your fear is a self-defence mechanism that you no longer need. You put it in place at a time when you were not ready to acknowledge whatever lies in the darkness that you now see before you. You are now ready to understand this thing and, in so doing, you will neutralize your fear.

6 Move forward as you affirm in your own words that nothing can harm you, and that you are in control at all times of your thoughts, feelings and actions. What is past is past. Now is the only reality.

7 You are likely to see something associated with your deepest fear (such as your death in a past life), but you are now merely an observer. And, once you have identified the source of your unease, it will dissipate like a bad dream and you will no longer be a prisoner of your own fears.

8 When you have returned to waking consciousness it is vital that you ground yourself in the usual way (see page 40). Then sit still for a few minutes to assimilate the experience.

Confronting a presence from the past

Seventy-five-year-old Maria had a morbid fear of the dark, which she was too embarrassed to confide to anybody. She would even find an excuse to wake her husband up in the night, so that she could go to the bathroom knowing that she could call him if her nerves failed her. She suspected that her fear originated in her adolescence, when she saw 'something disturbing' shortly after her father had died – a presence or a ghost. During her emotional journey she entered the darkness to revisit that day, but now she observed the spirit with detachment. She was able to acknowledge its existence as a genuine phenomenon, but without the irrational fear that had accompanied the original experience.

Sexual problems

Although most sexual difficulties are symptomatic of an emotional or physical problem with its origins in the present or recent past, there are rare occasions when the source of the problem may be traced to a former life.

Past-life repercussions

The most common cases are those in which the individual finds it difficult to commit to a long-term relationship, although there is no obvious reason for their reluctance. In regression it is likely that such people will discover they were betrayed by a lover in a former life, or forcibly separated from their lover by disapproving parents. Those who lost loved ones in tragic circumstances and vowed to remain faithful to their memory may also be unable to reconcile the idea of loving another; as a result, they may search from partner to partner in an unconscious attempt to reunite with their soul mate. In such cases regression can help to identify the source of the problem, but psychotherapy or counselling will also be needed to facilitate healing and closure.

If there is a trauma associated with the current problem, such as rape or abuse in a past life, it must be addressed by a qualified and experienced professional therapist or counsellor. In such cases it is not necessary for the therapist to believe in reincarnation, because they will regard the 'memory' as symbolic of a deep anxiety and their treatment will still be effective. However, it is not always simply a case of discovering that you were a victim and learning to forgive and move on. Occasionally you may learn to your horror that you were the perpetrator (for instance, the rapist) and it is your guilt that is causing conflict in your present relationships. Such revelations should, of course, be viewed with extreme caution, as they are impossible to prove beyond reasonable doubt; they may even be a false memory created unconsciously out of a need to express guilt for something else. The problem may be further complicated if regression reveals that you were a different gender in a past life. In such cases you will need to seek professional counselling or therapy to test the validity of these 'memories' and address the issues raised.

Another common difficulty arises when one partner is unable to enjoy a full physical relationship because they feel that sex is somehow 'wrong'. If there is no obvious cause (such as a recent unpleasant experience, religious restrictions or family conditioning), the answer may lie in a former life. It is not unusual to discover that the individual took a vow of celibacy as a member of a religious community, creating a conflict between physical desire and religious observance in the present incarnation.

Healing past-life sexual trauma

Trauma should always be treated by an experienced professional counsellor or therapist. However, the following exercise can be used as a supplement to the healing process.

1 Lie on a mat or bed in a foetal position, with your knees tucked into your chest.

2 Close your eyes and visualize your anger manifesting as a thick, black, oily substance in your solar plexus, your emotional centre.

3 Visualize it being drawn out through the skin, where it congeals, before drying and cracking like caked mud.

4 The places where you were touched by your violator are now being burnt away in the spiritual equivalent of a deep-cleansing treatment. The next moment the layer of impurities crumbles into a fine powder and is blown away into the ether. You are purged and cleansed.

5 Now imagine wrapping yourself in a thick, warm blanket to preserve the regenerative energy that is awakening within you, repairing the damage to your psyche and its physical counterpart.

Past lives and the subtle body

One of the least known, but most effective, methods of retrieving past-life memories involves focussing on each of the body's subtle energy centres (known as 'chakras') using the corresponding colours and phrases. By stimulating these centres you release any impressions associated with these areas of the body and their related functions, so that physical and emotional healing can take place.

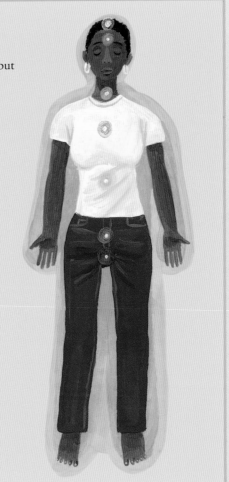

Chakras and colours

Initially you should work through all seven colours in turn, but in future you can choose to explore one aspect at a time.

1   When you feel comfortable and relaxed, visualize a red sphere located at the base of the spine. This is the Root Chakra. Red is the colour of physical energy and, as it is stimulated, you may feel a prickly sensation or heat in that area.

2   What personal associations do you have with the colour red? As a child, did you have a favourite toy of that colour, or a favourite item of clothing? Did your parents have a red car or a red house? Go back further now. Did your grandmother like red roses, or wear a red scarf? No matter how inconsequential they might at first appear, go back to your earliest memories.

3   You are now tuned to the level expressed in the phrase 'I have'. What impressions do you receive?

same incarnation. What is it? What emotions does it reawaken? Where are you?

6 Now continue in the same way, tuning into the other five chakras in turn, as follows: visualize a yellow sphere over the Spleen Chakra. This centre encapsulates your sense of identity, as expressed by the phrase 'I can'. What ambitions did you have in your former life? Were they frustrated or fulfilled? What knowledge and abilities have you brought with you from this past life?

7 Next visualize a luminous green sphere over the Heart Chakra, which is located in the centre of the chest. The corresponding phrase is 'I love'. What images arise? What memories and people from your past life do you associate with this phrase?

8 Now visualize a blue sphere expanding and contracting around the Throat Chakra. Blue symbolizes the quality of energy associated with communication and self-expression. The corresponding phrase is 'I say'. Visualize yourself engaged in conversation with someone from the scene in your previous existence. What are you saying to them? What would you like to say to them if you could go back there now? Is there something you (or they) are unable to express? Does it have a relevance to your present situation? Do you have unfinished business with this person? Do you know this person under another name in your present life?

9 Now visualize a vivid purple sphere over the Brow Chakra (also known as the Third Eye Chakra). This centre and its associated colour symbolize insight, intuition and ideas, as embodied in the phrase 'I see'. Is

4 Now absorb yourself in red – sink into it, as if it were a cloud of red mist, and feel yourself falling further and further down. When you emerge you find yourself in a scene from a former life, the life before your present incarnation. Where are you? There is something red that is of significance. What is it? What emotions does it reawaken? Who are you?

5 When you have explored this, visualize a pulsating orange sphere over the Sacral Chakra, beneath the navel. Don't simply imagine it – sense this subtle force whirling like a vortex, sending vital energy to revitalize and invigorate every cell of your being. Again, what personal associations do you have with this colour? Recall anything you can, to reawaken your earliest memories. You are now attuned to the centre whose energy finds expression in the phrase 'I feel'. Again, what impressions do you receive? Now absorb yourself in an orange mist and feel yourself free-falling further and further down. When you emerge, you see something orange from another former life, or possibly from the

there a window in that scene from a former life? If you are already outside, find a good vantage point and look down on that world. What do you see?

10 Finally, visualize a radiant sphere of white light over the Crown Chakra at the top of your head. The light is so brilliant and intense that it takes an effort to look into it, but you know you must. White is symbolic of your spiritual state as expressed in the phrase 'I am'. Find a mirror or a pool of water and look into it. Who are you? What have you learnt about yourself from this journey through the chakras?

How to read another person's past

If you want to practise reading the past life of a friend (you are too close to family members to get a reliable reading), you can use a variation on the previous exercise to help them explore past-life memories and release them for healing.

1 Sit opposite your subject and tune into each chakra in turn, as described above. Then extend your awareness outwards to tune into them, while you envisage the corresponding colour and phrase. What impressions do you receive at each level?

2 Take your time and trust your intuition. Tell your friend what you see, no matter how strange or unusual it might seem to you. You may be surprised at how accurate you are. However, you must be patient with yourself – it can be very difficult (even for experienced psychics) to give a reading for someone else, because clients tend to have unrealistic expectations, and the presence of an 'audience' may be intimidating.

CLEARING KARMA

Karma is the universal law of cause and effect. To put it simply, your every act – or failure to act – has a consequence. If you believe in karma, you cannot also believe in fate or predestination. You may think and react to certain situations in a predictable and habitual way, but karma states that you are in control of your life and can exercise your free will at any time to determine the course it takes.

Determining your own destiny

There is no supernatural agency involved; no omnipotent deity judging you or controlling the course of your life. You accumulate karma with every decision you make and, in so doing, you set in motion a sequence of events that affects the course of this life – and the next. For this reason it is self-defeating to attribute the good things in your life to luck, and the bad to the intervention of a

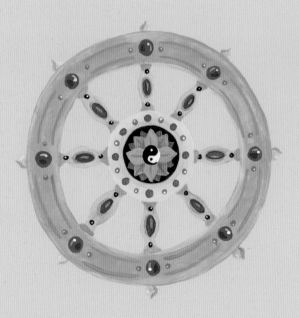

Things to remember

- It is a fallacy to think of karma as being either 'good' or 'bad'. It is neither. There is only karma (cause and effect).

- Contrary to popular belief, karma is not an exclusively Eastern concept. In Christianity it is expressed in the saying 'As you sow, so shall you reap' and in the directive 'Do unto others as you would have done unto you'.

- Karma is a dynamic that can be summed up in the Tibetan saying, 'If you want to know your past life, look into your present condition; if you want to know your future life, look at your present actions.'

- The Buddha said, 'What you are is what you have done, what you will be is what you do now'.

disapproving creator who is punishing you for 'past sins'. To see your life as a series of random events is to deny your Divine Nature and your power to determine your own destiny. You need to regard difficulties as something *you* unconsciously brought into being in order to learn something specific.

The law of karma is not always obvious, unless you make a conscious effort to become aware of it, because its effects are not always felt immediately. The results may be delayed for years, and sometimes even across several lifetimes. What makes it difficult for you to determine which of your problems are the result of past-life karma, or *karmic debt* and which are not, is the fact that karma is often cumulative. You may have neglected to do something that you could initially afford to ignore. However, over many years (or several lifetimes) this could set up a reaction that eventually creates a crisis that forces you to re-evaluate your life.

For example, an individual who takes advantage of their personal charm and business acumen to profit from another person's gullibility will inevitably fall victim to someone who plays on their over-confidence and does the same to them. Or a shrewd businessman who neglects his responsibilities may accumulate wealth, but then succumb to a heart attack; if he is fortunate, he may live to heed the lesson that his Higher Self is trying to teach him and come to realize the value of friends and family.

This is not sentimental, Hollywood-style moralizing – it is the way karma teaches us our obligations to ourselves and others, with our unconscious consent. But we have the free will to deny our Divine Nature and choose to ignore the lesson, in the hope of getting away with it. You may survive a crisis the first time and die laughing at what you got away with (which gives the impression there is no justice in this world), but karma dictates that you will be forced to face the consequences of your actions in the next life. However, you can learn how to *clear karmic debt* and deal with *unfinished karmic business* in this life.

A wonderful life

If you doubt the cumulative effect that one single act can have on other people's lives, rent a copy of Frank Capra's feel-good fantasy *It's A Wonderful Life*, starring James Stewart. Although it is overly sentimental, the film illustrates how one 'ordinary' person can influence the lives of everyone with whom he comes into contact, and how different their lives would have been, had he never lived.

Karma awareness exercise

You will begin to appreciate the consequences of karma if you follow the endless chain of cause and effect that results from a single, seemingly insignificant action, such as posting a letter.

1 By going to the post box you might have missed an important phone call that set off a chain of events. What might they have been? Or you might have encountered something on your way. If you had witnessed a minor road accident, would you have denied seeing anything so that you didn't have to make a statement? Or would you have offered to give your account to the police? And what might the consequences of those decisions have been, for you and for all those involved? Or you might have met a neighbour who boasted of having sold his house at an advantageous price, which encouraged you to put your property on the market. Again, what might the implications of such a decision be?

2 To follow another thread, consider the impact your letter might have, if it was an application for a job or a place at university, which you were subsequently offered (or denied).

3 Now, try following the chain of events using something that you did today, which might have had a serious effect on those involved. Then ask yourself why you should accept guilt for anything that you may have done, or neglected to do, in a past life – assuming you did what you thought was right at the time and that you could not have foreseen the implications of your actions.

Do you have a karmic debt?

If you want to find out whether you have incurred a karmic debt, you need to be prepared to ask yourself some pertinent questions and be scrupulously honest with your answers. This is not about making yourself feel good or bad, but about identifying real issues that are holding you back and that may be causing conflict in a relationship, so that all parties can achieve closure.

How to explore karmic debt

To establish whether you have a karmic debt, you can either work with an incident recovered during a regression session or use the following exercise.

1 Take a sheet of paper, or use a page in your journal, and allow your mind to become as blank as the paper.

2 Now make a list of people to whom you feel a vague sense of resentment, of whom you are jealous, or in whose company you simply feel uneasy. Perhaps there is someone with whom you disagree on principle or continually argue, because they seem to deliberately misunderstand you.

3 Write down a typical conversation that you have had with this person, then look for clues in your use of language. Ask yourself if there is a recurring theme, and what the source of that conflict might be.

4 There is no need to feel guilty for something you believe you may have done in a past life. First of all, despite all the checks you should make to verify your impressions, it is impossible to prove beyond reasonable doubt that what you have recovered is a genuine memory. It might have been a product of your imagination, influenced by something you read or saw that you still feel bad about; as a result, you may have recreated the experience to exorcise your guilt at not having been able to do anything about it at the time. It is also feasible that you have inadvertently picked up on something in the Collective Unconscious, which is not applicable to you at all. The only way you can be sure is to revisit the issue at a subsequent session and try to extract as many verifiable facts as you can.

5 Even if your memory is genuine, it may not have happened as you remember it. What you recall is coloured by your perspective,

distorted by the passage of time and influenced by factors that you cannot possibly be aware of (such as the history of your relationship with this person and the events that led up to this particular incident). In short, you must not judge yourself too harshly because you do not have all the facts. There may have been mitigating circumstances. If you cannot remember what you saw last week with absolute certainty, how can you trust something you retrieve from another lifetime? This is, of course, the argument at the heart of the case for regression, but while you can be sure that it is possible to recover genuine memories from the Unconscious, you cannot live your life in the shadow of a single incident, for the reasons already stated. Besides, even if what you recall is genuine and happened exactly as you remember it, *you* did not do this. Your past personality is responsible.

Although this personality and all that it experienced is a part of you, it is not the aspect that is currently to the fore. You have reincarnated to give yourself another chance, to learn from your 'mistakes' and to set right what you may have done in the past. There is no benefit in reliving the past – only in revisiting it for the purpose of restoring the balance so that you can move on.

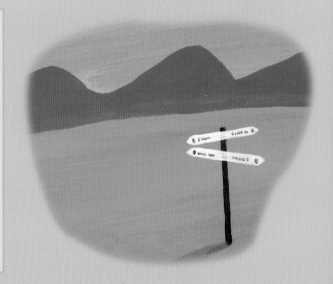

Things to remember

- The purpose of probing into past lives is to empower yourself to make the most of your present incarnation – *not* to dwell on the past.

- If you suspect that you have a tendency to assume the role of 'victim' or are given to occasional self-pity, you should avoid certain aspects of regression and consider consulting a qualified counsellor.

Clearing karmic debt

Having identified the person with whom you have incurred a karmic debt, and the nature of that debt, you are now in a position to clear it and move on. You can either choose to revisit that time in a hypnotic regression and alter the outcome by interacting with the other person in your trance, or you can reconnect with them on an unconscious level in a visualization.

Reconnecting on a psychic level

1 Begin by visualizing yourself sitting opposite an empty chair. You may wish to invoke your inner guide as moral support. If so, draw your guide to you in the usual way, through prayer or invocation, and sense it standing behind you, with its hands on your shoulders channelling energy to calm and centre you.

2 Now visualize the other person materializing in the empty chair. You are connected on a psychic level, which means that although the other party will not be conscious of this connection, they will experience the interaction either in a dream or in an idle moment while recollecting the past. It is not an imaginary scene designed to make you feel better – this connection will have real consequences.

3 Acknowledge the debt that exists between you, and state that you are aware it is holding both of you back from realizing your futures. Ask forgiveness (if this is

appropriate) and then sever the ties of etheric (psychic) energy that bind you together. Affirm that both of you are now free and that the negative thoughts and feelings you might have had are also in the past. It is no longer relevant who was right and who was wrong. It is time to let go of the past and move on. Wish the other person well in the future, and then ask for closure so that you can move on.

Rewriting your life script

Unless you are uncommonly independent and self-assured, you will have made many decisions based on what you thought would please other people – particularly your parents, peers, teachers and employers. By doing so, you will have become unconsciously conditioned to act and react in ways that you expected would bring you success, security and approval. This conditioned pattern of behaviour is known as your 'life script', and it is this – and not fate – that determines the course your life will take. However, your current life script is also influenced by your behaviour in previous lives. This compounds the conditioning, making it more difficult to alter it. But it can be done – or, rather, undone.

How to examine your life's course

If you want to know why your life has taken its present course, and how your past lives are continuing to influence your present, you need to do the following exercise.

1   Sit with a pad and pen in your hand. Take a few deep breaths and relax. Write a list of your regrets, beginning with the things you wish you had done, but didn't. Then list the things you believe you should have done differently. End with the opportunities that you didn't exploit, but wish you had. Leave a line between each item.

2   Now go through each list in turn and write 'why?' at the beginning of the blank line underneath. Then consider the implications of the action you took (or failed to take), and write a brief sentence outlining what happened to you as a result.

3   Do you see a pattern? Were your decisions influenced by one particular person? If so, why have you allowed that person to influence your actions to such an extent? Could there be a karmic debt between you?

4   Did something influence your choices? Was it fear or over-confidence? Could you sense the influence of past-life conditioning determining your course of action, or clouding your judgement?

5   Was the course you took really bad, or did it merely offer different opportunities? Did a similar choice present itself later on? Did you make the same decision the second time, or had you learnt from your earlier experience?

6   Now return to the first things you wrote. Close your eyes and imagine what might have happened in each case, had you made a different decision – the one you believe you *should* have made. Can you honestly say that your life would be better now? Would you really be more satisfied or fulfilled, had you taken a different route, committed to a different partner or accepted another job?

7   In counselling, modal verbs are forbidden. Words such as 'could', 'should' and 'ought to' are banned, because these imply that there is a right or wrong way. Past-life therapy is the same. You have *not* made mistakes – you have made decisions in this life and the last. These decisions have made you what you are today, and will determine what you will be tomorrow and beyond, in your future lives.

8   Can you accept that you made decisions in the past, based on what you felt or thought was right at the time? So you cannot criticise yourself for past 'mistakes', as a domineering parent or teacher might do. You are not following a curriculum designed to mould everyone to the same standard, or even to instil the same knowledge. Life is not an exam that you either pass or fail. You do not need to demonstrate the same understanding as everyone else. And you cannot make the 'right' decision every time. Consider this life a learning experience. Accept that you would learn nothing if you merely played a part in someone else's play. You are not reading from a script – you are writing one as you go along.

Karmic nightmares

Karmic nightmares are extremely rare, but can be triggered by a chance encounter with someone with whom you have unfinished business from a previous life. Alternatively, they may occur spontaneously when the Higher Self decides that you are ready to resolve these issues.

A nightmarish experience

Martin had a fascination with the early nineteenth century, which was so strong that it had influenced his choice of career. He became an historian, specializing in the English Regency period, although he could never identify what had inspired his interest. It was not until he reached middle age that he discovered the answer. One night he dreamt that he was a young pickpocket, who had been sentenced to death for petty crimes and was standing on the scaffold before a jeering mob. But it was more vivid than a dream – this was an overwhelming emotional experience; he was reliving a traumatic incident from a previous life. He awoke with a start, convinced that what he had experienced had been real. Afterwards he became an ardent opponent of capital punishment, of which he

had previously been in favour. He also mellowed into a more tolerant, even-tempered and compassionate person.

Clues to past-life karmic debts

In a conventional nightmare you might find yourself pursued by imagined enemies or in physical danger, as your fears take on symbolic form. But in a karmic nightmare you are likely to relive a significant incident from a former life with all the attendant emotions, because this issue is still 'active' as far as your Unconscious is concerned and may hold clues to a past-life karmic debt. Such dreams may explain why you have had an inexplicable dislike for someone you barely know, or why you harbour feelings of guilt, resentment or jealousy towards someone who hasn't given you cause to feel that way – at least in this life. But they should be seen as an opportunity to clear the issue and not as punishment meted out by a guilty conscience.

Each night, review the day in your mind with detachment and see if you can identify a pattern of behaviour that might offer clues to an unresolved issue from a former life. If you suspect there may be something, use 'The emotional journey' exercise (see pages 84–85) to clear it.

Exploring the karmic clues in a nightmare

If you experience a nightmare that you suspect may hold clues to a karmic debt, it is imperative that you note all the details in your dream journal immediately on waking. Then you can analyse the material at your leisure. Later, when you have a quiet moment, ask yourself the following questions.

1   Did the characters appear as fully formed personalities who assumed a life of their own – unlike the fantasy figures in a conventional dream, which are often composites of people you know or have seen during the day?

2   Did you recognize someone whom you knew in a former life, and did their appearance trigger a recollection of the nature of the debt between you?

3   Did you find yourself reliving a scene from that life and recalling the circumstances that bind you together?

4   Did this nightmare seem more real than a regular dream, and was it difficult to dismiss the images from your mind and the residual emotions on waking?

5   If so, this was because such nightmares are experienced in a heightened state of awareness – unlike a regular dream, which is created at the subconscious level and involves no more than the processing of images. In such a state, your connection with your Higher Self is at its strongest, and you are likely to awaken with both the solution and the will to resolve the matter, which your pride and ego would not have permitted in the days before the dream.

6   If, however, you are still troubled, you can return to the nightmare in a subsequent meditation and let the scenario unfold of its own accord. Or you can interact with the characters and listen to your own inner voice for the answers that you seek.

Unfinished business

Unfortunately life rarely ends as neatly as a novel or Hollywood movie. If there is unfinished karmic business nagging deep in your unconscious, you may carry it with you into your next incarnation like a wound that won't heal. If it involves another person who shares your sense of guilt or resentment, it could prove persistent and potentially damaging to your physical health and wellbeing, as you create a psychic bond with everyone with whom you come into contact.

Breaking the bonds

Although most of these relationships are transient and on a superficial level, a serious disagreement or injustice will bind you together from life to life, as you unconsciously recreate the situation that brought you together, until you resolve the karmic debt to your mutual benefit or learn to let go. If you are to be truly free, you need to be scrupulously honest with yourself and view the matter dispassionately in order to break the bonds that bind you to that person.

A debt beyond death

Karin had always been puzzled as to why John, a friend and supporter of her charity work, always seemed to turn up whenever she needed advice or practical help. It had occurred so often that she suspected that there must be a karmic link between them. However, it wasn't until she underwent a regression session that the connection was actually revealed. Under hypnosis Karin remembered a former life in which she and John were brother and sister, and she drowned herself after being abused by her employer. John had arrived too late to save her, but in the regression she saw him weeping over her body and heard him vowing to be there for her in the next life.

How to resolve unfinished business

If you suspect that you may have a karmic debt, the nature of your relationship to the other person should make obvious its origin and offer clues as to how you might resolve it. For example, if there is suspicion on either side, it suggests that there has been a betrayal of trust in a former incarnation; whereas if one of you seeks dominance over the other, or tries to belittle the other, this is indicative of residual resentment from an intimate relationship when you were lovers, siblings, or parent and child. However, it is not always necessary to identify the nature of a karmic debt in order for you to clear it. The following exercise will dissolve the psychic bond between you and the other person, by focussing on the link between your energy centres.

1 Visualize yourself sitting opposite the other person, with coloured strands connecting you at the following points: a red strand extends from the base of your spine to theirs; orange from your sacral centre to theirs; yellow from the solar plexus above your navel to theirs; green from the heart centre in the middle of your chest to theirs; blue from your throat centre to theirs; silver from the centre of your forehead to theirs; and a luminous white strand from your crown to theirs.

2 Now affirm in words of your own choosing – aloud or to yourself – that you release the other person from their karmic debt, that you have no unfinished business with that person (nor they with you), and that you wish them well on their journey through life.

3 Then see the various coloured strands withering and disintegrating like tendrils on a dying plant, one by one, concentrating particularly on the solar plexus centre, which is the focal point of your emotional energy.

4 Watch as the other person recedes into the distance, and know that you are both released.

The Karmic Court

Do not be discouraged from self-exploration and do-it-yourself past-life regression by the idea that you might have to struggle with serious psychological concepts. There is a shortcut that is not used by conventional therapists, but which has for centuries proven profoundly illuminating and practical for those seeking greater self-awareness and insight. This is an extension of pathworking (see pages 55–57), based on the idea that you can explore specific aspects of your own psyche by meditating on the kabbalistic Tree of Life (see the diagram on page 55).

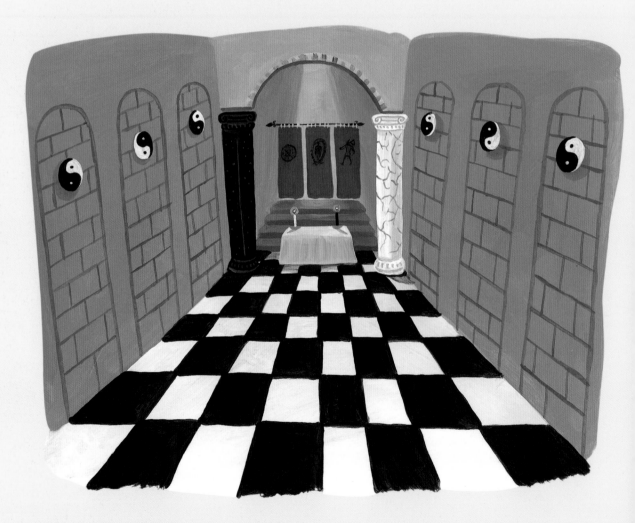

Taking an unresolved issue to the Karmic Court

This exercise is an example of how you can resolve a karmic conflict, clear your debt and sever your links to the other person, using a simple but highly effective visualization technique. The symbolism serves to attune you to the appropriate level of consciousness.

1 Close your eyes and visualize yourself in a small chamber or temple (the sphere of Malkhut on the Tree) with its floor of black and white chequered tiles symbolizing the complementary aspects of your personality and the governing principles of the universe.

2 You now stand before an altar flanked by two pillars: one of black onyx and the other of white marble. On the altar are two candles: one white and the other black. You represent the pillar of equilibrium, the balancing principle that seeks to create order from chaos. You are empowered with free will to bring this perfect state into being, and resolving conflict is one way in which you can bring this about.

3 Behind the altar are three doors, each of which is obscured by a curtain on which are depicted three tarot trumps. To your left is the Wheel of Fortune, the symbol of karma; to your right is the Fool, representing free will and self-determination; and in between is the card known as the World, symbolizing discrimination and discernment, the principal lessons of life.

4 Pass through the door to your left into a cloistered courtyard. Walk straight ahead until you come to the door of an inner temple. This is the temple of Learning (Hod). You enter and pass through this cathedral of knowledge, lined with books on all sides from floor to ceiling.

5 At the far end you exit into another cloistered walkway, at the end of which is the entrance to the temple you seek: Gevurah, the temple of Judgement. Inside you find a robed figure cradling an empty book in his arms.

6 As you stand before him he details the history of the karmic conflict existing between you and the other person. You are not being judged – this is merely a statement of facts. The robed figure is an archetypal aspect of your own personality, your Higher Self, and has your best interests at heart. Can you listen with impartiality? Can you appreciate the other person's perspective?

7 For the sake of your own growth and well-being, can you accept that there is no absolute truth, that right and wrong are subjective, and that there is no weakness in compassion or compromise? Affirm in words of your own choosing that you release yourself and the other person from the karmic bond that existed between you. Wish them well on their path through life, and thank the judge for presiding over the proceedings.

8 When you are ready, return to waking consciousness by counting down slowly from ten to one, then open your eyes. Sit still for a few moments until you feel grounded.

PSYCHICS AND GUIDES

While the exercises in this book can provide quite a lot of information about your past lives, you might also wish to consult a professional to help you put the pieces together or to deepen your insights. This chapter introduces the techniques practised by several types of psychics and guides. It aims to give you the information you need to make the best choice for your needs.

Getting professional help

Psychics and readers Professional psychics often feel that they have been born with an intuitive gift. They use a variety of techniques to aid their readings, such as cards and palmistry. Your own intuition is the best guide as to whether you should credit what a psychic tells you.

Regression therapists These practitioners are likely to have had professional training. Some have been trained in hypnotherapy; others in psychotherapy or counselling. Ask about the therapist's credentials. Unlike psychics, regression therapists aim to help you remember your own past lives, rather than sharing their psychic impressions of your past.

Soul-retrieval counsellors Drawing on the techniques of modern-day shamanism, these counsellors 'journey' with the aid of their spirit helpers to bring back a piece of your soul that may have been lost or hidden in the spirit world, as a result of a trauma you experienced in this life or a previous one.

Jungian counsellors Counsellors who draw on the work of psychologist Carl Jung (1875–1961) focus on helping you to understand the meaning of symbols and archetypes that may appear in your dreams or active imagination exercises. If you need help in interpreting significant past-life symbols, these counsellors can help.

Channellers These practitioners claim to receive messages about your past from spirit guides – disembodied entities such as the spirits of great teachers and sages. They can also help you get information about past lives by making contact with your Higher Self.

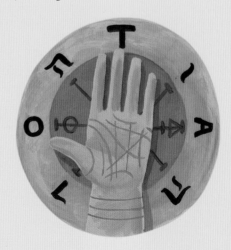

Consulting a psychic

There are valid alternatives to self-hypnosis, visualization and regression sessions, which can be equally effective in unearthing past-life impressions. One of these involves consulting a psychic. The only problems you might encounter are finding a psychic with whom you feel confident and accepting the fact that they (and not you) will be the source of information concerning your past lives.

How do you find a psychic?

Psychics who claim to be able to look beyond your physical appearance and 'read' the past-life impressions in your aura (the human energy field) are not as uncommon as you might imagine. Avoid the commercial psychic telephone lines and postal readings advertised in national magazines; instead, insist on a personal reading, face-to-face. That way you will get a better impression as to whether or not the psychic in question is genuine. Psychic fairs and conventions are a good place to observe and evaluate psychics before you commit yourself to a reading. But the best source is, of course, word-of-mouth recommendation.

One of the benefits of consulting a good psychic is that they should be able to describe a whole series of related lives to you in one reading. From that they should be able to reveal the underlying theme that links them together. In that way you can understand how you became who you are today, and what the main purpose of your present incarnation is. Such themes are extremely difficult to unearth in conventional regression sessions.

If you are serious about probing into your past lives on a long-term basis, you would do best to seek out a meditation and healing group or a fledgling (beginners') psychic circle. Such groups meet on a regular basis, usually at spiritualist churches, Quaker Meeting Houses and the like, where they offer support and advice to newcomers. They will know which psychics to recommend in the area.

What can you expect from a past-life reading?

Psychics work in many different ways. Some might tune into you by asking you to choose a flower from their garden when you arrive, so that they can pick up on your personal energy vibrations. Or they might ask to hold your watch or ring for the same purpose. This talent is known as psychometry (see page 52)

and often proves very effective in establishing a link between psychic and client.

Other psychics may ask to hold your hand, read your palm or make a random selection from a deck of tarot cards. However, this is usually no more than a device to give you confidence in their ability and put you at your ease. Cards, crystal balls and other paranormal paraphernalia serve as a distraction for the client and as a means of focus for psychics, who see what they need to see in their mind's eye, not in the actual object.

A genuine psychic will begin by giving you information about your present circumstances, and maybe even 'survival evidence' concerning a loved one who has passed over to the other side. This should give you confidence in their ability and help you to accept what follows. If this preliminary information is ambiguous or sounds as if it could be applicable to anyone, then you can be sceptical about whatever follows.

Be wary of those psychics who go on 'fishing expeditions' – looking for clues from you, which they can then elaborate upon. A genuinely gifted psychic will insist that you tell them nothing at all about yourself; they will also request that you answer only 'yes' or 'no' when they need confirmation that they are heading in a potentially fruitful direction. In the end, though, only you can judge as to whether the information you receive feels right and confirms what you had previously suspected.

One psychic's experiences

Psychic Jill Nash has given numerous revealing past-life readings in a career spanning almost 50 years. However, she has yet to encounter a client who had been a celebrated historical figure. 'The people who consult me are not expecting to find out if they were famous. They want to know why they are having certain problems at work or in their relationships. That's the real value of a past-life reading.

'I had one chap with whom I went back several lifetimes, because he had been pursued across the centuries by a woman who wouldn't let him be. They had a bitter dispute over money in a former life and she couldn't forgive him, which created a karmic bond

between them. I saw her in my mind as she appeared in her present incarnation and described her in considerable detail. His jaw dropped. "You've just described my ex-wife," he said.

'Another man challenged me to prove that reincarnation was true. He said that he'd had a reading some months before, and that he'd only believe it was true if I saw exactly the same thing. Undaunted, I tuned in and described a Persian market where he had been a trader in the thirteenth century. I could hear his sharp intake of breath as I detailed the surroundings and his dealings with the other merchants. "That's exactly what the other lady told me," he said.'

Jill likens the sensation she feels when giving a reading to flying backwards on a magic carpet. 'I take the client's hand in mine, so that I can tune into them, and then I'll feel as if I'm being carried backwards. When it's settled, I actually see them as they were at the time – and their surroundings. But it's not something I control. The information is given to me unconsciously by the client. I'm just the medium.'

Regression therapists

As we have seen, it is not necessary to consult a qualified regression therapist, but there are several advantages in doing so – the main one being that they will have the necessary counselling training, in the event that you are upset by any disturbing images or issues that you recall.

Tools of interpretation and integration

Regression therapists are trained to facilitate the recollection of past-life experiences that the client is not consciously aware of, and to help the client interpret and process the memories they recall during the session. Many therapists use hypnosis as a primary technique to induce deep relaxation, but some specialize in alternative techniques, such as bodywork, active imagination and shamanic journeys, which do not require their clients to enter a light trance. Professional regression therapists are effectively counsellors who specialize in identifying issues from a client's former life, and who then empower them to integrate the experience and insights into the present.

In contrast to hypnotherapy, where the client is open to positive suggestions in order to free themselves of fears, phobias and addictions, in regression therapy the client is in control at all times, with the therapist acting as a guide who is able to identify significant details and encourage the client to pursue them.

Hypnotic regression vs hypnotherapy

It is important to distinguish between hypnotic regression and hypnotherapy. Hypnotic regression involves putting someone in a trance-like state in which they can be regressed to an earlier stage in their life, or even further back to a former

Helpful tips

- It can be useful to make a short list of questions for the therapist, so that you can ensure that the session covers the themes you want to explore.

- If you are anxious, ask if you can bring a friend or family member to sit in on the session. Most therapists will have no objection, provided of course that the witness remains silent throughout.

- It is important to record the session onto tape so that you can later note what you said during the light trance-like state.

life, under the guidance of a hypnotist. Anyone can learn to be a hypnotist, and it is even possible to hypnotize yourself.

Hypnotherapy is a more serious undertaking. It must be entrusted to a fully qualified professional therapist, for whom hypnosis is one of a number of techniques for recovering repressed memories. These can then be worked on with a view to healing or increasing self-awareness.

Under the guidance of an experienced hypnotherapist, it is possible to identify, address and resolve issues such as addictions, phobias, eating disorders, sexual dysfunction and emotional blockages. In hypnotherapy the subject is usually aware of their surroundings and of the therapist's presence during the trance state. In contrast to conventional hypnosis, the client undergoing

hypnotherapy will receive only limited guidance from the therapist, to whom they will describe what they are seeing during the trance state.

Things to remember

- It is important to be aware that some hypnotherapists do not necessarily believe in reincarnation. Even those who do believe in it don't necessarily think it is possible to recover memories from a former existence.

- All hypnotherapists will treat your 'memories' as significant material from the Unconscious, even if they doubt their source.

A regression journey

When you consult a regression therapist, you might experience an exercise similar to the one outlined here. Remember that you are simply an observer of the scenes unfolding before you, and you will probably find them invaluable in helping to put your present life into perspective.

Travelling in time

You are now ready to experience your first solo past-life psychic regression session. You can perform this exercise either lying down or seated, but if you are lying on a bed or mat, remember to support your head with a pillow.

1   Make yourself comfortable, close your eyes and focus on your breathing. With every inhalation repeat the phrase 'Calm and centred' and with every exhalation repeat the phrase 'Deeply relaxed'.

2   Let your mind settle and your thoughts subside. Do not try to induce an experience. Simply let go and allow yourself to sink into a state of deep relaxation – as if you are settling into a warm, scented bath.

3   When you feel suitably relaxed, visualize yourself enveloped in a white mist. It is so dense that you cannot see beyond it. Looking down, all you can see are your feet. The mist clears just enough to reveal that you are standing at the top of a spiral staircase. The lower steps are obscured by the mist. Steady yourself by gripping the handrail to your right, and count aloud as you descend: 'One ... I am relaxed and ready ... two ... going down ... three ...

deeper ... four ... deeper ... five ... down and round ... six ... going deeper ... seven ... deeper down ... eight ... relaxed and ready ... nine ... deeper ... ten ... down.'

4   You have now reached the bottom of the staircase, but all you can see are your feet and the ground. What type of footwear (if any) are you wearing? What kind of ground are you standing on? The mist begins to clear. You are in a landscape that is strangely familiar. Do you recognize this place? Can you tell which country it is, from the scenery or plants? What season is it? Are there any clues as to what period you might be in? What feelings do you associate with this place?

5   Feel free to explore, knowing that you can return at any moment you choose. Are there any buildings nearby? If so, are you attracted to one in particular? Approach the entrance. Did you live or work here? If not,

Things to remember

- During a regression there is no need to be anxious. You are in control at all times. If you feel uneasy for any reason, simply return to waking consciousness by counting down from ten to one.

what did you do here? Who were your neighbours? What is your abiding memory of this place?

6 Go inside and look around. Have no fear. No one can harm you. You have returned because there is something of significance for you here. What is it?

7 Is there a mirror or a basin of water in which you can see your reflection? What clues can you find to your identity? Is it a period when there might be photographs, or a portrait?

8 If this is a place you knew in a former life, you should know what is around the next corner. Test your memory by trying to find specific rooms. Perhaps there is a skill that you used to practise in a particular room, or a device that you operated? If so, can you locate it and recall how it works?

9 Perhaps you were a person of importance, and this place holds a clue as to why you feel under-appreciated in your present life. Or perhaps something bad happened here, and you left this life bearing resentment towards someone. If so, return with the details so that you can address the issue at a later date, but leave the emotions behind. If there is a basin of water nearby, plunge your hands into it and let the residue of your emotional energy dissolve in the water. If not, clutch an object and discharge the negative energy into this.

10 When you are ready, return to waking consciousness in the usual way.

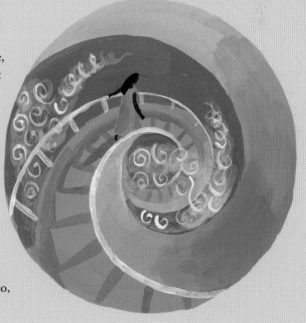

Soul-retrieval experts

Soul-retrieval experts are modern-day shamans. The shamanic view holds that, in terms of energy, everything that has ever happened exists in an eternal now. Thus, to a shaman, your entire past – including your past lives – exists energetically within your present life.

Freeing a lost soul

During a traumatic event, a piece of your soul (here understood as your vital life essence) may sometimes break away or get trapped in the past event. Soul loss can occur as a result of the tragic death of a parent or separation from a loved one, or because of an accident, a rape or an episode of physical or emotional abuse. In psychological terms, what happens is that you dissociate from a part of yourself so that you can survive whatever is happening to you. Problems occur when the lost-soul part does not return after you recover, or when it is unable to return due to the nature of the trauma.

A soul-retrieval counsellor uses shamanic techniques, such as drumming, dancing, rituals or chanting, to induce a trance through which to 'journey' – often with the help of guiding spirits – to the place where this trauma is still occurring for you. The goal is to find the part of your life force that has been caught in that event and to 'blow' or 'sing' it back to your energetic body.

When the soul-loss trauma involves the death of a loved one, a piece of your soul can be trapped by the spirit of the deceased person. Soul retrieval can release such holdings and help the deceased person find peace as well. However, such shamanic healing needs time and care, for the process can be emotionally difficult. Follow-up sessions of therapy are often needed to help you reintegrate the retrieved parts of your soul so that they do not split off again.

A soul lost in childhood

A woman whose grandfather had been abusive to her grew increasingly angry and depressed months after her grandfather's death. A soul-retrieval counsellor journeyed to the grandfather's spirit and discovered that, when the grandfather was a little boy, he had been abused by his own mother. When the counsellor helped the grandfather regain the piece of his soul that had been lost in childhood, he released the part of his granddaughter's soul he had been holding.

Can soul-retrieval help you?

There are a number of symptoms that may point to soul loss. Read through the following list and see whether any of these signs apply to you. If you have experienced several of them, you may benefit from consulting a professionally trained soul-retrieval counsellor for advice.

1 Do you often feel that you are observing life as an outsider, rather than being engaged or involved with people and events?

2 Do you feel 'spaced out' a lot of the time?

3 Do you often feel 'empty' or as if 'something is missing'?

4 Has a loved one described you as 'detached' or 'emotionally unavailable'?

5 Do you suffer from pervasive fears?

6 Do you often feel angry with the world?

7 Do you have difficulty focussing your will to make things happen?

8 Does your life feel dream-like, or not quite real?

9 Do you find it difficult to trust people?

10 Do you have unexplained feelings of sadness or grief?

11 Do you suffer from a chronic illness or debilitating health condition?

12 Have you been diagnosed with, or treated for, depression?

13 Are there periods of your life that you simply cannot remember? Have you encountered similar blank spaces in your exploration of a past life?

Jungian counsellors

The Swiss analytical psychologist Carl Jung advanced the theory that many of our anxieties arise from a feeling that we are incomplete, that we lack a sense of identity and so are seekers in search of our true selves. In order to reintegrate the complementary aspects of our psyche, we need to understand the significance of the symbols and archetypes that inhabit our dreams, and connect with what he called the Collective Unconscious, or Universal Mind – a matrix of mental energy containing the

sum of all human experience. To do this he developed a technique known as 'active imagination' in which the individual can access knowledge and experience from a former life in a guided visualization. If you need help in interpreting significant past-life symbols, Jungian counsellors who practise this technique may well be able to help you.

Jung's archetypes

Historical figures such as Napoleon and Cleopatra continue to hold a fascination for us because they are archetypes (the embodiment of certain human qualities to which we all aspire). Napoleon personified the quality of the self-made man whose intuitive abilities brought victory, despite seemingly insurmountable odds. Cleopatra personified beauty and guile, as well as serving as an iconographic image of an exotic and distant place, to which we would all like to escape from time to time.

The eccentric who believes himself to be Napoleon has become a comic cliché. Unfortunately there are many otherwise perfectly sane people who have deluded themselves into believing that they have been the diminutive Frenchman (or an equally celebrated historical figure) in a previous incarnation, based on their experiences of regression. If you question the basis for their belief, they become passionately defensive because, for them, the experience was real. That is a trap you need to be wary of when you are undergoing regression, if you are not to fall prey to self-deception.

You may tell yourself that you would never allow yourself to be deluded into believing you had been such a famous figure in a former life. However,

the problem is that we all have such archetypes in our psyche, and other archetypes do not always appear in such a blatant manner.

The symbolism of different archetypes

To avoid confusing an archetype with a genuine personality from one of your past lives, you need to consider their appearance and actions. With experience and a little common sense, it can be done. One clue is that archetypes, by definition, appear as the embodiment of a specific aspect of human nature and not as a rounded, complex personality. They act out the role assigned to them.

The archetypes

Anima The personification of the intuitive and emotional aspects of our personality, often seen as the female attributes. It is symbolized by the Mother, the Princess, the Amazon and the Priestess.

Animus The personification of the practical and rational aspects of our personality, often seen as the male attributes. It is symbolized by the Father, the Hero, the Youth and the Magician.

Wicked Queen or Witch Symbolizes the over-protective and possessive aspect of our nature.

Wise Man Symbolic of inspiration and insight. If this figure appears in a regression or vision, you should give special significance to its advice.

Actor/Actress The appearance of this archetype indicates that you are considering developing or revealing a previously hidden aspect of your personality. By bringing it on to the virtual stage in your vision, you are seeking approval from the conscious mind.

Artist/Composer/Poet Symbolizes your creative impulse. Its appearance suggests that you could be suppressing your self-expression and that you need to overcome these doubts.

Child Represents your own inner child or ego, which can indicate wilfulness, innocence or potential. Its actions and attitude in a regression should make it clear which of these it symbolizes.

Jailer/Persecutor/Judge It is not uncommon to see this figure during a regression and to assume that you were at one time persecuted for your belief, or subjected to a grave injustice. However, although it is possible that you did experience an incident of this nature, the appearance of this archetype could be purely symbolic of a guilty conscience. Serious and objective analysis should reveal the true significance of this image.

King and Queen/Emperor and Empress The personification of parents, and of your own potential and desire to rise above the ordinary and mundane.

Monks If you are actively seeking answers and meaning in your present life, it is likely that you had a series of earlier incarnations with a strong religious or spiritual theme, most probably as a monk or nun. However, if there is no resonance or recognition on your part, the figure is almost certainly symbolic of self-discipline and devotion.

Native peoples Although it is highly likely that the appearance of so-called 'primitive people' in your regression or vision represents a real memory, they can symbolize anything that is unknown, but also attractive to you.

Pursuer Again, this figure might be from your past, but you will have to trust your intuition to reveal the truth. If there is no emotional connection, it suggests that your pursuer is a symbol of your shadow self – an aspect of your personality that you have denied. To assimilate it you will need to re-enter a meditative state and visualize whoever has been chasing you in your vision. Then see yourself stopping and facing them: demand to know what they want from you. That should be sufficient to reveal the reason for their appearance.

A counsellor's experiences

American hypnotherapist and counsellor Jeanne Philips offers her clients hypnotic regression, but only if they request it.

'Often a client who has come to me for counselling will ask to be regressed at some point during treatment because they suspect that the root of their problem lies in a past life. It is not something that I actively promote and I never try to persuade them that they need it. But if they express an eagerness to go deeper with someone they have come to trust, I can take them to a place where they feel safe and secure.

'I have been regressed by some of the most eminent experts in the field. I know how traumatic it can be, but if a suppressed memory needs to be cleared then regression is the safest and most effective method of processing it.

When I was regressed I re-experienced my death in the gas chamber of a Nazi concentration camp. I watched my parents suffocating before my eyes. I wasn't a mere observer, I was reliving it. But afterwards I felt I had released something that had been a burden – that had oppressed me all of my life. I lost my fear of death, abandonment and of being terrorized and bullied.

'Exploring past lives is part of our instinctive need to understand who we are and why we think and behave in the way we do. We need to forgive so that we can move on. Clinging to the past and reliving a former injustice only serves to damage the individual who cannot clear it.

'A good example of this was a client who would unconsciously wreck all of her relationships. She couldn't give herself fully to anyone. As a child she had suffered abuse and had been abandoned by her alcoholic mother. Counselling wasn't enough so I regressed her to a point where she re-experienced life in the womb. At that stage she remembered that her mother had tried to commit suicide because she hadn't got over the loss of her first child. She heard the doctors talking about her mother's precarious mental state and the risk she was running with her second pregnancy. She felt her mother's anguish and came out of the regression feeling sorry for her mother and realizing that her mother had blamed her for having to live through more pain.

'In a subsequent session she relived a former life in which she had been the sole survivor of a massacre and had spent the remainder of her life alone in the mountains. She emerged from the regression feeling free for the first time in her life and she understood why she had difficulty relating to other people. That was enough to begin the process of healing.'

Tattwa symbolism

Modern regression techniques are designed to recover personal memories from a previous incarnation, but there is an alternative, little-known method for accessing a random moment in time from our collective past.

Doorways to the past

According to the Irish poet and mystic W. B. Yeats, who experimented with this technique during the 1890s, there are certain magical symbols of obscure Eastern origin that can trigger an altered state of consciousness. These make it possible to experience other realities, including the past. Yeats claimed that such a feat is possible because our individual memory is part of an infinite reserve of memories, which mystics call the Akashic Records. This archive does not, of course, exist as a physical reality, but as a matrix of mental energy upon which we impress our thoughts and experiences. As fanciful as it might sound, the concept is accepted in principle by many modern psychologists, who refer to it as the Collective Unconscious.

How to make Tattwa cards

You can make your own set of Tattwa cards (as this vehicle to an altered state of consciousness is known) and test their effectiveness.

1   Cut five squares from a sheet of stiff black art board, making them just slightly larger than a standard playing card. On the face of each card paint one of the following shapes: a red triangle, a yellow square, a silver horned moon, a light blue circle and a purple oval. Alternatively, you could cut these shapes from coloured paper and stick them on.

2   Once you have your set of finished cards, choose one at random. Then lie down and stare at the shape until it is fixed in your mind. Turn the card over. The same shape should now appear in a complementary colour.

3   Now close your eyes and internalize the image, just as you would the afterglow of a candle flame during meditation. Visualize the shape growing gradually until it envelops you, then see yourself stepping through it.

4   Don't forget to record what you see on the other side.

Channelling

If you require irrefutable evidence of past lives, why not ask for it in writing? Incredible though it may seem, it is possible to question your Higher Self and receive a direct answer that will provide you with all the facts you need.

How to channel for yourself

1 Sit with a notepad and a pen in your lap. Close your eyes and visualize the blank sheet of paper in front of you. Now say the following sentence to yourself: 'I am open and receptive to recollections from my former lives. Which memory do I need today to heighten my insight and understanding?'

2 Wait for a minute, allowing thoughts and impressions from the past to bubble up from the Unconscious. Then open your eyes and write down whatever came into your mind. If you receive what appears to be nonsense, write it down anyway, as this is all part of the clearing and connection process. Do not analyse what you receive or you risk blocking the flow.

3 If you receive an uninterrupted deluge of thoughts (known as a 'stream of consciousness'), continue writing until it comes to a natural conclusion. Otherwise, close your eyes and repeat the sentence.

4 Do this 22 times for 11 days in succession, if necessary, before taking a break of 11 days. However, you can expect a breakthrough long before then. If there is something that your Higher Self has been trying to communicate for some time, you may even make a connection the first time you attempt the exercise. However, don't be disappointed if it takes several attempts.

5 When you make the connection with the Unconscious, you will know it is genuine because you will find yourself scribbling faster than you can think about what you are writing.

Assessing the evidence

Whether you undergo a psychic reading or a regression session with a professional therapist, you need to be rigorously honest with yourself when evaluating your experience.

Things to remember

- If there is ever an attempt by the psychic, guide or therapist to establish a sexual relationship, or if they make inappropriate remarks, you must end the session immediately.

Self-assessment

Before you consider what to do next, ask yourself the following questions:

1 Were there any verifiable facts in the details the psychic or guide gave me? Can I find proof for anything that I was told, or was it mainly generalities that could apply to anyone?

2 Can I relate to any of the information given to me? For example, did the session reveal the root of a phobia, the reason for my attraction to someone, or why a place strikes a chord with me? Had I told them about this issue before they revealed the cause?

3 Did the recovered memories feel right for me? Did they ring true deep inside, or did they sound like romantic fiction?

4 Did I have the impression that the therapist was saying what they thought I wanted to hear?

5 Was there a sense that they were trying to flatter me or feed my fantasies?

6 Did they reveal unpleasant truths that resonated within and made me emotional, without understanding why?

7 Did they exert any pressure on me to commit myself to further sessions, or hint that if I didn't return I might suffer negative effects?

8 Did they appear to have my well-being at heart, or was there an effort to make me feel that I would be lost without their help?

9 Did I feel that they were competent and confident in dealing with past lives? Or was there a suspicion that they were only offering this service to accommodate their client's wishes or to earn extra income?

After-effects

People react differently to regression and psychic readings. In general you can expect to feel a deep contentment, having made a connection with a lost aspect of yourself. You may even feel relief – as if a burden has been lifted from your shoulders. However, other potential reactions may occur and are described below.

If your expectations are not fulfilled ...

If you leave a session feeling disappointed, it could be because you had unrealistic expectations of the therapist or of the process itself. Were you hoping to be told you had been someone special, but instead discovered that you had led a series of routine lives? If that is the case, you may need to question your motives for seeking therapy. Is there a possibility you are a 'therapy junkie', seeking solutions and support because there is something lacking in your present circumstances? If you can acknowledge that, there isn't a serious problem. In fact, it is a sign of increasing self-awareness if you can identify your motives and address the issues.

Of course, your disappointment may originate with the therapist or reader, if they revealed nothing of value. It is possible they may even have been using the session to pursue their own agenda, or to prove their own personal theories and beliefs. In that case, put it down to experience and try again with another psychic or guide when you are ready.

If you feel depressed ...

If you come away from a session feeling depressed, it suggests that the session unearthed other issues, which may have more to do with your recent past than with a former existence. These issues need to be addressed by a professional counsellor or therapist. Do not try to deal with serious problems on your own, even if you have been brought up to believe that you should handle your own affairs. You can exacerbate a problem if you keep it to yourself and brood upon it or, worse, deny it. You could drive it further into the Unconscious, where it will influence your future moods, thoughts and behaviour. It is better

to share your reaction with someone who is qualified to address emotional issues, and who will be empathic and non-judgemental.

If you feel worse before you feel better ...

It is not uncommon to feel this way – this is often the case with complementary therapies, which are holistic in nature. This means that they address the person as a whole and seek the source of the 'disease', rather than simply curing the physical symptoms. In exploring your psyche, the therapist may have released memories and emotions that have been suppressed for years (perhaps even over many lifetimes). Such deep healing can bring the memory of bad experiences back in the form of nightmares or psychosomatic physical symptoms (see page 72), although these will usually ease within a few days or a week.

Transference

Although regression and psychic readings have the potential to deal with serious spiritual, psychological and emotional issues, there is no iron-clad guarantee that whatever is recovered was, in fact, experienced by you in a former life. It is possible for you to have made an empathic link with the therapist or reader, and to have acquired a false memory under their influence (whether or not this was intentional on their behalf).

It is also possible – though highly unlikely – for the therapist to have confused their own past-life experiences or false memories with those they have attributed to you. This is known as 'transference' and should be considered a possibility, so that you do not unquestioningly take on guilt due to the therapist's influence (unconscious or otherwise).

Things to remember

- The purpose of regression therapy is to lead you towards self-realization and acceptance of yourself, as you are now.

- You will undermine the benefits of regression if you castigate yourself for past 'mistakes', over which you have no influence and which you cannot now undo, other than by living a decent and happy life.

Index

Acknowledgements

Executive Editor **Brenda Rosen**

Managing Editor **Clare Churly**

Executive Art Editor **Sally Bond**

Designers **Pia Ingham & Annika Skoog for Cobalt Id**

Illustrator **David Dean**

Production Controller **Simone Nauerth**